At Issue

Book Banning

Other Books in the At Issue Series:

At Issue

| Book Banning

Ronnie D. Lankford, Book Editor

GREENHAVEN PRESS

An imprint of Thomson Gale, a part of The Thomson Corporation

Detroit • New York • San Francisco • New Haven, Conn. • Waterville, Maine • London

Christine Nasso, *Publisher*
Elizabeth Des Chenes, *Managing Editor*

For more information, contact:
Greenhaven Press
27500 Drake Rd.
Farmington Hills, MI 48331-3535
Or you can visit our Internet site at http://www.gale.com

LIBRARY OF CONGRESS CATALOGING-IN-PUBLICATION DATA

Book banning / Ronnie D. Lankford, book editor.
        p. cm. -- (At issue)
    Includes bibliographical references and index.
    ISBN-13: 978-0-7377-3783-7 (hardcover)
    ISBN-13: 978-0-7377-3784-4 (pbk.)
    1. Censorship. 2. Challenged books. I. Lankford, Ronald D., 1962-
    Z657.B73 2008
    363.31--dc22
                                                                    2007028834

ISBN-10: 0-7377-3783-2 (hardcover)
ISBN-10: 0-7377-3784-0 (pbk.)

Printed in the United States of America
10 9 8 7 6 5 4 3 2 1

Contents

Introduction

The battle over banning books has a long history, one that actively continues into the twenty-first century. Throughout history, governments and religious bodies have attempted to ban books that presented ideas considered revolutionary and/or blasphemous. The Catholic Church issued the *Index Librorum Prohibitorum* (List of Banned Books) in 1529, a list that continued to grow until Pope Paul VI abolished it in 1966. As the Catholic Church's political power waned following the Renaissance, European governments continued the practice of banning books.

The battle over banning books also has a long history in the United States. On March 3, 1873, the Comstock Laws (the Federal Anti-Obscenity Act) were enacted, leading to the suppression of classic books including Aristophanes' *Lysistrata*, Chaucer's *Canterbury Tales*, and Boccaccio's *Decameron*. Mark Twain's *Huckleberry Finn* was banned from a Concord, Massachusetts's library in 1885, while Walt Whitman's *Leaves of Grass* was deemed as too provocative for publication in Boston in 1881. During the 1960s, censorship battles raged over D. H. Lawrence's *Lady Chatterley's Lover* and Henry Miller's *Tropic of Cancer*.

Who Bans Books?

Today, the Catholic Church and national governments seldom lead battles over banning books. Instead, most people first learn about book banning on the local level. But who exactly attempts to ban books? On the local and state level, the battle plays out in communities, school boards, public libraries, and state legislatures. But these battles can still rage on the national level and around the world, involving governments, corporations, book publishers, and private citizens.

Local and State Book Bans

Most attempts to ban books take place on a local and, occasionally, state level. Here, issues are usually resolved by local government bodies and have no effect on other localities. Often a battle starts over a controversial book, and a local resident will submit a challenge to have the book banned from the school curriculum or library shelf. In 1989, two school districts in California banned *Little Red Riding Hood* because the protagonist had brought wine to her grandmother. In 2005, the state of Oklahoma attempted to ban books with homosexual themes from the children's section of public libraries.

In 2006, the American Library Association (ALA) received notification of 546 book challenges in libraries and schools. The same year, *And Tango Makes Three* by Justin Richardson and Peter Parnell topped the ALA's list of most frequently challenged books in the United States. The book tells the story of two male penguins who parent a mixed-sex couple's egg, and critics considered the book pro-homosexual and anti-family. Cecily Von Ziegesar's *Gossip Girls* and Phyllis Reynolds Naylor's *Alice* were also at the top of ALA's banned books' list for 2006.

National Book Bans
in Western Democracies

While Western democracies are generally considered sympathetic to free speech and a free press, books continue to be banned in Germany, the United States, Canada, France, and Australia. Australian customs siezed Nicholas Saunders's *E for Ecstasy* in 1994, and the United States outlawed disseminating information on illegal drugs in the Methamphetamine Anti-Proliferation Act of 1999 (though *E for Ecstasy* remained legal in the U.S.). Canada prosecuted Ernst Zündel under two different laws for publishing *Did Six Million Die?* in 1974, a book denying the Holocaust. In the spring of 2007 in the United

States, a federal court blocked the publication of a 500-page manuscript by Danny B. Stillman to be titled *Inside China's Nuclear Weapons Program* because the CIA claimed the book disclosed classified information.

Banning or censoring books also occurs on the corporate level and within state textbook committees. In 2004, comedian-writer Jon Stewart published *America (The Book)* and Wal-Mart refused to stock the book in its retail stores. In the case of textbooks, censorship is often subtler, with textbook committees eliminating material that may be considered ideologically offensive before publication. Textbook committees, however, also have the power to decline books, as when the Texas State Board of Education rejected *Environmental Science: Creating a Sustainable Future* by Daniel D. Chiras in 2001, in effect banning the book from Texas classrooms. All of these methods restrict a book's availability and content, and in some cases, withdraw a book from circulation.

Book Banning Around the World

While censorship is considered relatively mild in most Western democracies, many governments around the world openly ban books. *The Bible* is banned in many Muslim countries, though Saudi Arabia has allowed tourists to carry a personal copy. In Iran, bans have prohibited popular books like Dan Brown's *The Da Vinci Code* along with the works of many native authors. Writers have also been jailed, beaten, hospitalized, and murdered around the world for expressing views that deviate from their government's. Huang Xiang, who immigrated to the United States in 1997, served 12 years in Chinese prisons and work camps; Hrant Dink, a Turkish-Armenian writer, was murdered in January 2007.

Many attempts to ban books and/or silence authors also cross national borders. One of the most notorious cases revolved around author Salman Rushdie's *Satanic Verses*, published in September 1988. Muslim leaders found the book offensive, leading the spiritual leader of Iran, the Ayatollah Ruhollah Khomeini, to offer a reward for Rushdie's assissination. While Rushdie went into hiding and escaped injury, radical Muslims firebombed bookstores, burned copies of *Satanic Verses*, and injured or killed persons involved in the translation of the novel.

The Contemporary Debate

In the heat of these battles, many realize that it is nearly impossible to suppress a book, even when everyone agrees that a book should be banned. While two school districts in California may ban *Little Red Riding Hood*, the book may still be available in nearby districts. While Rushdie's *Satanic Verses* may be difficult to obtain in the Middle East, it remains easily available in the United States and Europe. Likewise, if a textbook is banned from Texas schools, it may still be used in Virginia. All-encompassing book bans seem unfeasible.

Nonetheless, frequent attempts to ban books in both the United States and around the world continue. Within these conflicts, cultures define themselves. Is it better to suppress provocative information, or does suppressing information limit freedom of speech and freedom of the press? Is it better to suppress hate speech and politically incorrect views from young readers, or is it better to allow young readers the freedom to study these issues and reach individual conclusions? The authors of the articles in *At Issue: Banned Books* explore these questions and more in this volume. That these questions remain so contentious attests to the power of books, even in a computer age, to carry influential and contested ideas.

Book Banning Has Legal Limits

Claire Mullally

Claire Mullally has practiced law in New York City and Nash-ville for 12 years, and specializes in intellectual-property law.

In the 1982 Pico *decision, the U.S. Supreme Court set limits on book banning in school libraries. Book banning by secular and religious bodies has a long history. Following the invention of the printing press in 1450, however, it became more difficult to eliminate an offensive book. European governments nonetheless attempted to keep books considered heretical or radical out of circulation by forbidding publishers to print them. Following in Europe's footsteps, Americans like Anthony Comstock attempted to ban books for moral reasons. While the Comstock Law began to break down during the early 20⁰ century, school libraries con-tinue to censor classic literature like Mark Twain's* The Adven-tures of Huckleberry Finn. *While books may still be banned under the* Pico *decision, they cannot be removed to prohibit the dissemination of ideas.*

"Local school boards may not remove books from school library shelves simply because they dislike the ideas contained in those books. . . ."
—U.S. Supreme Court in Board of Education,
Island Trees School District v. Pico (1982)

Claire Mullally, "Banned Books: Overview," *First Amendment Center,* www.firstamend mentcenter.org, January 4, 2007. Reproduced by permission.

The *Pico* case is the most important court decision to date concerning school libraries and the First Amendment. In it, the Court recognized that the First Amendment rights of students are "directly and sharply implicated" when a book is removed from a school library. Therefore, the discretion of school boards to remove books from school libraries is limited. The law requires that if a book is to be removed, an inquiry must be made as to the motivation and intention of the party calling for its removal. If the party's intention is to deny students access to ideas with which the party disagrees, it is a violation of the First Amendment. . . .

Early Book Banning History

Book-banning in school libraries is only the latest battleground in a centuries-old war over the censorship of ideas. Secular and religious authorities have censored books for as long as people have been writing them. In 360 B.C., Plato described the ideal Republic: "Our first business will be to supervise the making of fables and legends; rejecting all which are unsatisfactory."

Censorship followed the European settlers to America.

In ancient times, when hand-scribed books existed in only one or a few copies, destroying them (usually by burning) guaranteed that no one would ever read them. Once the invention of the printing press around 1450 made it possible to circulate many copies of a book, book-burning, though still highly symbolic, could no longer effectively control the dissemination of texts.

Twenty years after Johann Gutenberg's invention, the first popular books were printed and sold in Germany; within another 20 years, Germany's first official censorship office was established when a local archbishop pleaded with town officials to censor "dangerous publications." In England, Henry

VIII established a licensing system requiring printers to submit all manuscripts to Church of England authorities for approval and in 1529, he outlawed all imported publications. In 1535, the French king Francis I issued an edict prohibiting the printing of books. By 1559, in reaction to the spread of Protestantism and scientific inquiry, the Roman Catholic Church issued the *Index Librorum Prohibitorum*, likely the first published and most notorious list of forbidden books. The purpose of the *Index* was to guide secular censors in their decisions as to which publications to allow and which to prohibit, since printers were not free to publish books without official permission. At a time when society was dominated by religion, religious and secular censorship were indistinguishable. The Catholic Church continued to print this *Index*, which grew to 5,000 titles, until 1966, when Pope Paul VI terminated the publication.

Censorship followed the European settlers to America. In 1650, a religious pamphlet by William Pynchon was confiscated by Puritan authorities in Massachusetts, condemned by the General Court and burned by the public executioner in the Boston marketplace. The incident is considered to be the first book-burning in America.

The pioneer of modern American censorship was Anthony Comstock, who founded the New York Society for the Suppression of Vice in 1872. In 1873, using slogans such as "Morals, not art and literature," he convinced Congress to pass a law, thereafter known as the "Comstock Law," banning the mailing of materials found to be "lewd, indecent, filthy or obscene." Between 1874 and 1915, as special agent of the U.S. Post Office, he is estimated to have confiscated 120 tons of printed works. Under his reign, 3,500 people were prosecuted although only about 350 were convicted. Books banned by Comstock included many classics: Chaucer's *Canterbury Tales, The Arabian Nights*, and Aristophanes' *Lysistrata*. Authors whose works were subsequently censored under the Comstock

Law include Ernest Hemingway, James Joyce, F. Scott Fitzgerald, Victor Hugo, D. H. Lawrence, John Steinbeck, Eugene O'Neill and many others whose works are now deemed to be classics of literature.

People trying to ban books from libraries do not usually regard their efforts as censorship.

Paul Boyer, in *Purity in Print: Book Censorship in America from the Gilded Age to the Computer Age*, claims that the Comstock Law merely formalized what had been a "gentleman's agreement" among publishers, booksellers and librarians enforcing a Victorian "code" of literary propriety. In the 1920s, nationally publicized court battles over such novels as James Joyce's *Ulysses*, began to erode this code. The frightening specter of the Nazi book-burnings in Germany in 1933, Boyer says, crystallized anti-censorship sentiment in the United States. Within a few months after the book-burnings in Germany, the landmark federal court decision in *United States v. One Book Called "Ulysses"* clearing *Ulysses* broke the back of the Comstock Law.

Book Banning Now

Despite the lessons of the past, incidents of book-banning have continued to the present. Many of the most recent incidents occur at a local level, in public schools and libraries.

Henry Reichman, in *Censorship and Selection: Issues and Answers for Schools*, defines censorship as: "[T]he removal, suppression, or restricted circulation of literary, artistic or educational material—of images, ideas and information—on the grounds that these are morally or otherwise objectionable in light of standards applied by the censor."

People trying to ban books from libraries do not usually regard their efforts as censorship. A member of the community, school board member or parent objects to, or "challenges," a book, requesting its removal or sequestration so that students may not have free access to it. Most frequently, books are challenged because they contain profanity or violence, sex or sex education, homosexuality, witchcraft and the occult, "secular humanism" or "new age" philosophies, portrayals of rebellious children, or "politically incorrect," racist or sexist language. The American Library Association has documented more than 6,000 such challenges in the United States between 1990 and 2000.

If enough people protest the challenge, the book may not be removed. But sometimes no one notices: A book is removed and stays lost to a school or community. Sometimes a parent, community member or even a librarian fearing controversy will quietly remove the book from the shelf. It is impossible to document and quantify this form of "stealth censorship." Judith F. Krug, the American Library Association's [ALA] director of the Office for Intellectual Freedom, estimates that for every recorded book challenge, as many as four or five challenges go unreported.

Classic literature such as Mark Twain's *The Adventures of Huckleberry Finn* and John Steinbeck's *Of Mice and Men* were among the top 10 most frequently challenged books from 1990 to 2000, according to the ALA's Office for Intellectual Freedom. Of the 448 recorded challenges in 2001 (down from 646 in 2000), the most often challenged were those in the Harry Potter series, for its focus on wizardry and magic and "Satanic influence."

The *Pico* Decision

In 1975, several members of the school board from the Island Trees School District on Long Island, N.Y., obtained a list of books deemed "objectionable" by Parents of New York United, a conservative organization. The board determined that the district's school libraries contained several titles on the list: *The Fixer*, by Bernard Malamud; *Slaughterhouse Five*, by Kurt

Vonnegut Jr.; *The Naked Ape*, by Desmond Morris; *Down These Mean Streets*, by Piri Thomas; *Best Short Stories of Negro Writers*, edited by Langston Hughes; *Go Ask Alice*, authorship anonymous; *Laughing Boy*, by Oliver LaFarge; *Black Boy*, by Richard Wright; *A Hero Ain't Nothin' But a Sandwich*, by Alice Childress; *Soul on Ice*, by Eldridge Cleaver; and *A Reader for Writers*, edited by Jerome Archer.

The school district's established policy required the school superintendent to appoint a review committee upon a receipt of a complaint about a book. Nevertheless, the board members arranged to have the books "unofficially" removed from the libraries without appointing a committee.

When word of its actions reached the news media, the board issued a press release that characterized the books as "anti-American, anti-Christian, anti-Semitic and just plain filthy." They said the books contained "obscenities, blasphemies, brutality and perversion beyond description," and concluded that "it is our duty, our moral obligation, to protect the children in our schools from this moral danger as surely as from physical and medical dangers."

A committee later appointed by the superintendent determined that several of the books should be placed back on the shelves. The board rejected the recommendations of the committee and again ordered that the books be removed. Steven Pico, a 17-year-old high school student, led a group of students who sued the board in U.S. District Court, claiming a denial of their First Amendment rights. The district court found in favor of the board, citing "respect for the traditional values of the community and deference to a school board's substantial control over educational content." The students appealed to the 2nd U.S. Circuit Court of Appeals, which reversed the decision and sent the case back to the district court for trial. The school board then appealed to the U.S. Supreme Court.

A closely divided Supreme Court ruled 5 to 4 in favor of the students. Writing for the plurality, Justice William Brennan reasoned that the First Amendment right to *express* ideas must be supported by an implied right to *receive* information and ideas. While school officials do have significant authority to control the content of speech in schools, that power is not absolute: "'. . . students may not be regarded as closed-circuit recipients of only that which the State chooses to communicate.'" School officials "cannot suppress 'expressions of feeling with which they do not wish to contend.'"

Brennan noted that the "special characteristics of the school library make that environment especially appropriate for the recognition of the First Amendment rights of students." Nevertheless, he emphasized that his decision was a narrow one, limited to the *removal* of books from a school library, and not extending to the *acquisition* of books or their use in the school curriculum. Brennan also recognized that local school boards had "broad discretion in the management of school affairs," and said that if a board acted solely upon the "educational suitability" of the books in question or solely because the books were "pervasively vulgar," such actions would not be unconstitutional.

Since *Pico*, First Amendment litigation involving book censorship in schools has usually turned on the rights of a school board to control classroom curricula by prohibiting the use of certain texts and/or an inquiry into whether a certain challenged text is "vulgar."

In 1989, the 11th U.S. Circuit Court of Appeals upheld a Florida school board's removal of a previously approved classroom text because of its perceived vulgarity and sexual explicitness (*Virgil v. School Board of Columbia County*). Interestingly enough, the high school literature textbook was banned because it contained selections from Aristophanes' *Lysistrata* and Chaucer's *The Miller's Tale*, two authors whose works were among the thousands banned under the Comstock Law in the late 19th century.

2

Book Censorship Is a Universal Practice

Boyd Tonkin

Boyd Tonkin is a literary editor for the Independent.

Censors, seeking to silence authors whose writings they disapprove of, have gone so far as to assassinate them. Many previously banned books still hold their power to disturb, and while a minority of readers will advocate the complete freedom of the press, nearly everyone approves of some form of censorship. Even libertarians, for instance, approve of surveillance that allows law enforcement to track child pornographers. Only when it comes to the depiction of sexuality does the 20th century seem more lenient than its historical predecessors. Overall, the advance of history has only shown that different eras may adopt a previously banned book as a classic and ban a previously approved book as provocative.

George Bernard Shaw once wrote that assassination is the ultimate form of censorship. That hardly counted as a joke 100 years ago. Now, it sounds like no more than a footnote to today's headlines. A month ago, the Turkish-Armenian editor Hrant Dink died at an ultra-nationalist assassin's hands. His murder came after a sustained, high-level campaign to vilify and prosecute those writers—such as Dink, or Turkey's Nobel laureate Orhan Pamuk—who dare openly to debate the Ottoman massacres of a million or more Armenians in 1915.

Just three months earlier, the author and journalist Anna Politkovskaya paid the same price, shot in the lift of her Moscow apartment block after her dogged and fearless research into the underside of Putin's regime had made her one ruthless foe too many. As for the grotesque public killing, so far unsolved, of Alexander Litvinenko in London last November: remember that the former KGB agent's chief offence, in the eyes of his Russian enemies, was to publish a book that denounced the alleged terror tactics of his ex-employers in provoking the second Chechen war. That book, *Blowing Up Russia*, was promptly and permanently banned in his native land. . . .

At home, freedom of expression hardly looks in better shape. Last year, only a concerted campaign by what one minister once sneeringly called "the comics lobby"—in fact, a very broad coalition of writers ,artists, lawyers, parliamentarians, and (yes) entertainers—reined in an ill-drafted catch-all law against the incitement of so-called "religious hatred." The same government that devised that measure looked on in silence as several existing laws were broken when a hooligan gang claiming to act for the Sikh community forcibly shut down the Birmingham Rep's production of Behtzi (Dishonour) by the young British writer Gurpreet Kaur Bhatti. "No one from the Home Office was prepared to defend the playwright," noted the National Theatre's director Nicholas Hytner, "even after she was threatened."

Our politicians seem to have concluded that there are no votes in artistic freedom, or even upholding the law, but many in pandering to every angry cry of "offence."

Almost two decades ago, British publishers stood firm against the Ayatollah Khomeini's fatwa and issued a joint paperback edition of *The Satanic Verses* in solidarity with Salman Rushdie. Would the same collective support take shape now? Much of the media has decided to engage in "responsible" self-censorship that often feels not too far from cowardice. No UK publication, channel or station (save for a couple of rapidly squashed student magazines) allowed its readers or viewers to make up their own minds about the Danish cartoons of Mohamed.

In many cultures, free expression remains truly a matter of life and death, quite as risky as it ever was. So *The Independent's* collection of once-banned books arrives at a crucial moment. From Vladimir Nabokov's *Lolita*, to Hubert Selby's *Last Exit to Brooklyn*, from Henry Miller's *Tropic of Cancer* to William Burroughs' *The Naked Lunch*, it brings together 25 landmark works that still have the power to disturb and to confront that led to their initial battles with authority.

[W]e all approve of censorship in one form or another.

Recall (just for starters) that Nabokov's "nymphet" is not around 14, as many people think, when she catches the predatory eye of Humbert Humbert. In fact, she is 12. Anthony Burgess's *A Clockwork Orange* satirises the currents in modern society that give rise to the random violence of disaffected kids. At the time, some read his critique as an endorsement of thugs. Many might still do so today.

Champions of patriotic warfare will still be affronted by Erich Maria Remarque's *All Quiet on the Western Front*. Haters of political spin and guile will be appalled by Machiavelli's *The Prince*. Believers in the spotless innocence of youth will be disgusted by Edmund White's *A Boy's Own Story*. Partisans of Castro's just and equal Cuba will be outraged by Reinaldo Arenas' *Singing from the Well*. Islamic patriarchs will be repelled by Taslima Nasrin's *Shame*. Feminist puritans will be distressed by DH Lawrence's *Lady Chatterley's Lover*—and so, explosively, on.

"Literature", as the poet Ezra Pound put it (and his own flaky Fascist tendencies have expelled his work from many college courses over recent years), "is news that stays news".

This selection of fearless and visionary works has stood the test of time. They retain the right to shock—and awe.

Some readers may indulge in a little superior scorn when they consider the bourgeois prudery that sought to suppress *Madame Bovary's* adulterous passion, or the apartheid-era racism that tried to crush the compassion and solidarity of Alan Paton's *Cry, the Beloved Country.*

Look at the history of our current "cultural wars," and you find that even the bravest standard-bearers of liberty had their blind spots when it came to censorship.

But, of course, we all approve of censorship in one form or another. Modern politicians in fragile multicultural societies seek control over material that "offends" organised blocs of voters. Many liberally minded people feel glad that British laws passed over recent decades forbid inflammatory racist speech, writing and images. The casual clubland asides of a generation back can now lead straight into court—as the BNP's Nick Griffin recently found out. Fresh legislation against the "glorification" of terrorism, aimed at jihadi hotheads but couched in terms that could have ensnared 1980s supporters of the ANC, has few vocal or visible opponents. Those for whom Holocaust denial represents a uniquely vile assault on truth welcome the legal shaming of David Irving—though not, to be fair, his jailing in a hypocritical Austria.

Not even extreme libertarians will raise a finger or a voice against the extension of surveillance powers of the law-enforcement agencies who aim to eradicate child pornography via large-scale trawls such as Operation Ore. Here is a vast network of hi-tech censorship that all but violent criminals support. Overall, it seems as if everyone in Britain now agrees with the provocative US critic Stanley Fish, who in the 1990s wrote an influential anti-liberal tract entitled *There's No Such Thing as Free Speech—And It's a Good Thing Too.* For Fish, as for other radicals who make common cause with conservatives, all expression takes place within a contested set of rules and constraints—psychological, verbal, social, economic. And only fantasists ignorant of history and humanity ever believe in a blank slate.

Look at the history of our current "culture wars", and you find that even the bravest standard-bearers of liberty had their blind spots when it came to censorship. John Milton's 1644 pamphlet *Areopagitica* remains the most forceful English blast in favour of the unsupervised freedom to publish. It claims that killing a book is as bad as killing a man, for "who kills a man kills a reasonable creature, God's image; but he who destroys a good book kills reason itself, kills the image of God, as it were, in the eye". Note Milton's qualification, "good": the first in a long line of provisos with which free-speech champions sought to head off the menace of proscription via an appeal to moral or artistic merit. Fast-forward to 1960: the successful arguments of Penguin Books in the *Lady Chatterley* trial still turned on the "literary value" defence allowed by the Obscene Publications Act.

Our shibboleths and scapegoats will no doubt look as bizarre to future critics as the passions of the past so often do to us.

As many fair-weather libertarians do today, Milton also had a sticking-point: Roman Catholicism. Catholic propaganda, he thought, exempted itself from the protection that the state ought to offer authorship because it amounted to treason: a deep-rooted attack on the values of the nation and its culture. So, too, for many liberals now. The fascist or the racist puts himself outside the free-speech pale, and so deserves ostracism or punishment. American mainstream thinkers said the same of Communists in the McCarthy era. Now, a young Islamist radical who holds up a scrawled banner calling for the beheading of some infidel may face a charge of incitement to murder.

Only in one disputed territory—the depiction in print of sexual acts—does the early 21st-century in the West seem significantly more permissive an age than those preceding it. Even here, anomalies and arguments abound. Christian campaigners, not long ago, tried to enforce the removal of mass-market British editions of books by the Marquis de Sade. If filmed, many of Sade's more grossly sadistic scenes (which sometimes involve children) would be instantly deleted once the BBFC had taken a look. Why, protesters asked, are legislators sure that images can harm but words do not? And even words can still run foul of British law. One maverick Manchester publisher, Savoy Books, endured a tireless 17-year campaign of legal harassment by local police and magistrates. Their onslaught culminated in the confiscation and destruction of David Britton's gruesome satirical fantasy, *Lord Horror*. This was the last major suppression of a British printed work for supposed obscenity, overturned only after a long process of appeal in 1992.

Besides, authoritarian societies—from the Rome of Augustus to the Cuba of Castro—have often bothered much less about escapist erotica than about literary challenges to the power of the state and the person of its leaders. George Orwell knew his history when he filled the "Airstrip One" of *Nineteen Eighty-Four* with cheap gin and cheap porn to pacify the proles. Trend-setters of the 1960s liked to believe in the "subversive" power of sexuality on page, screen or stage. A century earlier, they would have had a point: witness the scandal of Baudelaire's *Les Fleurs du Mal*, and, indeed, the prosecution of *Madame Bovary*. In the interwar years, British law still proudly made an ass of itself by, absurdly, putting works such as Radclyffe Hall's tortured lesbian romance *The Well of Loneliness* in the dock.

After the *Lady Chatterley* trial, the floodgates formally opened—but the creative well dried up. In fast-buck mass culture, the "sexual intercourse" that began for Philip Larkin "in 1963" soon felt more like a cheap trick than a new dawn. Only among gay authors in the West did written sex hang on to its edge of danger and defiance—from Edmund White in the US and Reinaldo Arenas in Cuba to Jean Genet in France. The Old Bailey conviction of *Last Exit to Brooklyn* in 1967 (overturned after an appeal led by John Mortimer) surely bucked the Sixties liberal trend because of the gay and transsexual milieu of much of Selby's novel. Meanwhile, in the 1970s, James Kirkup's poem for *Gay News*—in which a Roman soldier erotically contemplates the crucified Jesus—brought the laws of blasphemous libel out of their ancient mothballs. That case, too, resulted in a conviction.

Reading the great banned books of other times and other climes will hardly sort out the dilemmas and contradictions that recur in the history of public speech. It might, though, help us to understand that the sands of taboo and transgression, of heresy and blasphemy, are forever shifting under our feet. Within a generation (to take just two obvious examples), Joyce's *Ulysses* and Lawrence's *The Rainbow* moved from being proscribed to being prescribed—from the magistrates' court to the seminar room. Other novels travel in the contrary direction. In 1900, Harriet Beecher Stowe's anti-slavery saga *Uncle Tom's Cabin* seemed to millions one of the noblest, most influential books since the *Bible*. By 2000, it had become a byword for patronising ignorance. Our shibboleths and scapegoats will no doubt look as bizarre to future critics as the passions of the past so often do to us.

So read these formidable literary pariahs with an eye on our age, as well as theirs. In olden days a glimpse of stocking was looked on as something shocking—but, otherwise, Cole Porter got it wrong. Heaven knows, anything definitely doesn't go these days. The prudes and persecutors have simply changed tack and chosen different ground, as they always have.

"Let there be light," say writers. In answer, the powers that be treat them not as the salt of the earth but as a law unto themselves, merely concerned with filthy lucre. All those phrases, as it happens, come from a much-censored author: from William Tyndale's magnificent English translations of the *Old* and *New Testaments*, which have left a deeper mark on everyday English speech than any other text. And what happened to Tyndale? The Catholic authorities, not content with burning his heretical work, burned him at the stake in Flanders in 1536. In cultures where the written word is banned and burned—even forbidden versions of the *Bible*—then living men and women will often follow. Ask the grieving family and colleagues of Hrant Dink.

Censuring the Censors: Writers Speak Out

'Many a man lives a burden to the earth; but a good book is the precious life-blood of a master spirit, embalmed and treasured up on a purpose beyond life. . . We should be wary therefore. . . how we spill the seasoned life of man preserved and stored up in books; since we see a kind of homicide may be thus committed, sometimes a martyrdom, and if it extend to the whole impression, a kind of massacre.' *John Milton, Areopagitica, 1644.*

'Nature knows no indecencies; man invents them.' *Mark Twain, Notebook, 1896.*

'If we don't believe in freedom of expression for people we despise, we don't believe in it at all.' *Noam Chomsky.*

'The peculiar evil of silencing the expression of opinion is, that it is robbing the human race; posterity as well as the existing generation; those who dissent from the opinion, still more than those who hold it. If the opinion is right, they are deprived of the opportunity of exchanging error for truth; if wrong, they lose what is almost as great a benefit, the clearer perception and livelier impression of truth, produced by its collision with error.' *John Stuart Mill, On Liberty, 1859.*

'The dirtiest book of all is the expurgated book.' *Walt Whitman.*

'The fact is that we are willing enough to praise freedom when she is safely tucked away in the past. In the present . . . we get nervous about her, and admit censorship.' *E.M. Forster, The Tercentenary of the "Areopagitica," 1944.*

'Censorship is never over for those who have experienced it. It is a brand on the imagination that affects the individual who has suffered it, for ever.' *Nadine Gordimer, Censorship and Its Afermath, 1990.*

'Wherever they burn books they will also, in the end, burn human beings.' *Heinrich Heine, Almansor, 1821.*

'A censor pronouncing a ban, whether on an obscene spectacle or a derisive imitation, is like a man trying to stop his penis from standing up. . . The spectacle is ridiculous, so ridiculous that he is soon a victim not only of his unruly member but of pointing fingers, laughing voices. That is why the institution of censorship has to surround itself with secondary bans on the infringement of its dignity.' *J.M. Coetzee, Giving Offence: Essays on Censorship, 1994.*

'Books won't stay banned. They won't burn. Ideas won't go to jail. In the long run of history, the censor and the inquisitor have always lost. The only weapon against bad ideas is better ideas.' *Alfred Whitney Griswold, The New York Times, 1959.*

'All censorships exist to prevent anyone from challenging current conceptions and existing institutions. All progress is initiated by challenging current conceptions, and executed by supplanting existing institutions. Consequently, the first condition of progress is the removal of censorships.' *George Bernard Shaw, Annajanska, 1919.*

'We have a natural right to make use of our pens as of our tongue, at our peril, risk and hazard.' *Voltaire, Dictionnaire Philosophique, 1764.*

'Woe to that nation whose literature is cut short by force. This is not merely interference with freedom of the press but the sealing up of a nation's heart, the excision of its memory.' *Alexander Solzhenitsyn, Nobel Prize Acceptance Speech, 1972.*

'You can never know what your words may turn out to mean for yourself or someone else; or what the world they make will be like. Anything could happen. The problem with silence is that we know exactly what it will be like.' *Hanif Kureishi, Loose Tongues, 2003.*

'If some books are deemed most baneful and their sale forbid, how then with deadlier facts, not dreams of doting men? Those whom books will hurt will not be proof against events. Events, not books should be banned.' *Herman Melville, The Encantadas, 1856.*

'If a man is a fool the best thing to do is to encourage him to advertise the fact by speaking.' *Woodrow Wilson, Address to the Institute of France, 1919.*

'Free speech is the whole thing, the whole ball game. Free speech is life itself.' *Salman Rushdie, The Guardian, 1990.*

'The liberty of the press is a blessing when we are inclined to write against others, and a calamity when we find ourselves overborne by the multitude of our assailants.' *Samuel Johnson, The Lives of the Poets, 1781.*

'Our liberty depends on the freedom of the press, and that cannot be limited without being lost.' *Thomas Jefferson, Letter to James Currie, 1786.*

'The press is not only free, it is powerful. That power is ours. It is the proudest that man can enjoy.' *Benjamin Disraeli.*

'He that would make his own liberty secure, must guard even his enemy from opposition; for if he violates this duty he establishes a precedent that will reach himself.' *Thomas Paine, Common Sense, 1776.*

'I believe there are more instances of the abridgment of the freedom of the people by gradual and silent encroachments of those in power than by violent and sudden usurpations.' *James Madison.*

3

Banned Books Week Is Hypocritical

Stephanie Beckett

Stephanie Beckett is an aerospace engineer and Plan II student at the University of Texas.

Banned Books Week has a major flaw: some books should be removed from libraries. Parents can regulate what a child reads at home, but they can no longer provide oversight when a child goes to school. While no parent is able to control a child's behavior at all times, schools cause parental concern when they allow children access to inappropriate materials. Complete intellectual freedom may be acceptable at academic libraries, but school libraries must take into account that many issues are too complex for children to understand. Banned Books Week is less about celebrating intellectual freedom than demonizing concerned parents.

Last week was Banned Books Week, which annually raises awareness about the grave threat that book banning poses to our civil liberties. And surely everyone would agree that the government shouldn't restrict our rights to read whatever we darn well please.

But Banned Books Week is not a protest of governmental book banning, because such book banning does not actually exist in our nation. Instead, the week, sponsored by the American Library Association [ALA], seems to be a movement to stop private citizens from asking certain library collections to remove certain books from the shelves.

Banned Books Week is thus silly, because some books should be banned from certain libraries. Also, these requests by private citizens (or "challenges," as the ALA calls them) actually just add to the public debate about books—the challenges certainly do not amount to censorship.

Most challenges are made because the challenger believes that a book has offensive language or sexually explicit material. The vast majority (71 percent) of these challenges are made about books in primary or secondary schools or school libraries.

One reason school is such a headache for good parents is that parents have practically no control over what their children are doing during the school day. Parents hand their kids off to the educational system and just hope that the schools are monitoring their kids' behaviors just as the parents would.

Parents need to look out for kids, and this extends to the ability of parents to help guide their kids' reading material.

So if a school library has a book that the parent does not approve of, this is a major problem for parental control. Parents obviously don't have control over every aspect of their children's lives, and kids will of course pick up information that is inappropriate for a child's ears. But, there's no reason for schools to compound this problem even further by providing, for example, sexually explicit material or books with obscene language.

Take as an example the book that was the most-challenged in the United States last year [2005]: an illustrated, cheerful-looking book, *It's Perfectly Normal: Changing Bodies, Growing Up, Sex, and Sexual Health.* The book is supposedly for ages 10 and up, so it may be found at an elementary school near you. But, can you blame parents for wanting their elementary school-aged kids to learn about sex in a supervised manner rather than by independently reading a (rather graphically illustrated) sex education primer?

Perhaps it is unacceptable for any book to be banned from a general purpose public library or a library in academia unless the book is clearly illegal (such as child porn). But in school libraries, it's a different matter altogether. Children don't have all the same rights as adults—they can't smoke, drink or give consent to have sex with an adult. These restrictions on children take into account the fact that kids are immature and too inexperienced to understand the complexity of certain issues.

Parents need to look out for kids, and this extends to the ability of parents to help guide their kids' reading material. Observant and concerned parents can do this at public libraries, but at school libraries kids do not receive parental guidance. School library collections should reflect that.

It would obviously be wrong for every challenge to end in the banning of a book from a library, even a school library. After all, if challenges universally led to book banning, books that just have unpopular opinions would end up becoming unavailable for public consumption.

But most challenges do not actually result in the book being banned in a particular collection. Instead, the challenges are simply formal written complaints that are made by concerned citizens. Banned Books Week's goal is thus really just to label people as uncultured, narrow-minded and generally un-American if they are concerned that a book is inappropriate for a particular library collection.

How else would the stakeholders of public education (children's parents) monitor the book collection of a school library if not through official complaints? Surely the ALA doesn't believe that all possible reading materials, such as clearly pornographic books, should be included in school library collections. And yet, without any kind of community involvement like the challenging process, school libraries could include just about anything in their collection that any particular librarian deemed appropriate.

The truly disheartening thing about Banned Books Week, though, is that, by trying to demonize the legitimate concerns of private citizens, it undermines the true viciousness of nations that actually do ban books.

Banned Books Week Supports First Amendment Rights

Neva Chonin

Neva Chonin is a pop music critic for the San Francisco Chronicle.

People who really care about the availability of quality books should express concern over banned and challenged books all year long. Many of the books on the banned and challenged lists are classics, and the reasons for challenging many of these books are absurd. Young readers are smart enough to understand complex and controversial subjects. In truth, people who challenge and ban books are afraid of the ideas that these books contain. Unless people with broader views support the freedom to read all year around, society will suffer.

"If all printers were determined not to print anything till they were sure it would offend nobody, there would be very little printed."—Benjamin Franklin.

Why can't Johnny read? Because we won't let him. The 25th anniversary of Banned Books Week just ended, but don't tell me we're going to concern ourselves about this issue only one week out of 52. If nothing else, the censored-book list is comic gold, if you're at the point where you consider the human race a lost cause, which I kinda have, but that's another topic for a later column . . . or maybe that's at the heart of all my columns. Huh. Is there a psychiatrist in the house?

Sorry. The books, the books. The American Library Association (ala.org) and others keep lists of the most challenged and banned books, and these lists are something to see. Incidentally, "banned" and "challenged" are not synonymous: First comes the challenge ("We shouldn't expose kids to *Lassie Come Home* because it promotes running away to solve problems"); only if the challenge succeeds is the book removed from libraries and/or classrooms.

The selection of offending texts is horrible and funny and horribly funny. I suppose I can understand why wing-nut evangelicals might object to the wizardry of Harry Potter, or why some African American groups might bristle at the racist, but realistic, language in *The Adventures of Huckleberry Finn*, or how feminists could take umbrage at the (unsympathetic) misogyny of *American Psycho*. But someone needs to explain why anyone needs protection from *James and the Giant Peach* or *A Wrinkle in Time*.

OK, it's true that Roald Dahl's *James and the Giant Peach* depicts juvenile disobedience and death by squashing (it's hard to control a giant peach). And yes, Madeleine L'Engle's *A Wrinkle in Time* contains a lot of quasi-Christian spirituality, though less so than *The Chronicles of Narnia* (also often challenged). But seriously, if there's anyone with a case for how these fictional elements would dement otherwise normal kids, I'd like to hear it. (I'd also like to see someone squashed by a giant peach, but dude, that's just the dementia talking.)

The Most Challenged Books

On and on go the lists, veering from unfathomable to knee-slapping to just plain depressing. The award for writer most frequently challenged belongs to Judy Blume, author of such subversive works as *Are You There, God? It's Me, Margaret*, the tale of a girl and her period. Spreading the word about puberty, man. It's the biggest slide on the devil's playground. Other famously idiotic challenges include *Anne Frank: The Di-*

ary of a Young Girl for its Blume-esque discussion of adolescence and because some parents just consider the story of a Jewish teenager in Nazi-occupied Europe "a real downer."

There are no words to argue with such logic. There are also no words, or at least there are words crossed out, in some schools when it comes time to teach Ray Bradbury's *Fahrenheit 451*. Words like "hell" and "damn" and such. Here I must cough discreetly and remind readers that *Fahrenheit 451* is about censorship and book burning as a means of controlling the populace. And so . . . well.

Let's continue. According to the ALA, parents in Nevada's Washoe County successfully banned Shakespeare productions from their schools, citing the Bard's "language and sexual innuendo." Parents are busy elsewhere, too. They've challenged Shel Silverstein at least twice—for *Where the Sidewalk Ends* ("promoting cannibalism") and for *A Light in the Attic* ("encourages children to break dishes so they won't have to dry them"). They've sought to ban Maurice Sendak's *In the Night Kitchen* for an illustration showing a bare-butt kid and L. Frank Baum's *The Wonderful Wizard of Oz* for its occult content. Here's my personal favorite: DeleteCensorship.org reports that Mary O'Hara's *My Friend Flicka* was removed from an elementary school reading list for calling a female dog a "bitch." Oh, the things parents will do to protect The Children™.

Some censorship is self-defeating. Consider Germany's stupidity in banning Adolf Hitler's *Mein Kampf*, as if that country could erase its Nazi past by banning its written history. (La la la, Adolf, they can't hear you.) Harper Lee's treatise against bigotry, *To Kill a Mockingbird*, has been challenged for its use of racial slurs, and Harriet Beecher Stowe's *Uncle Tom's Cabin* has gone from being banned for its "anti-slavery propaganda" to being banned for its "undesirable racial language."

Returning to my earlier quandary, please explain, gentle readers, why anyone, child or adult, requires protection from these books? Do self-righteous censors genuinely think that reading anti-racist literature that dutifully reflects the language of racists will damage a black kid? That reading about menstruation will damage adolescent girls? For that matter, that any well-adjusted human being would devolve into a drooling anti-Semite through exposure to Hitler's ponderous ruminations or become a religious fanatic by seeing spiritual metaphors in a fantasy novel?

My opinion? Many censors don't believe any of this. They ban books for a simpler reason: They don't like these books' ideas, and they don't want anyone else to like them either. Whether right-wing fundamentalists or twittering New Age solipsists, they long for a world that's more a padded cell than a shifting vista. They are focused, fanatical and single-minded. And baby, unless those of us with slightly broader views of life dig our heels in and treat every week as Banned Books week, we're all going to be sharing that padded cell with them.

5

Book Banning Violates Children and Young Adult Freedoms

Jim Trelease

Jim Trelease is the author of The Read-Aloud Handbook.

Although everyone should have the right to protest in a free society, that right has limitations: no one should be allowed to impinge on someone else's freedoms. Sometimes, a book may be inappropriate for one grade level, but suitable for another. Similarly, books inappropriate for the classroom should still be collected in public and school libraries as well as the home. While there are cases in which censorship may make sense (if a book is racist, for example), many censors attack non-harmful books like J. K. Rowling's Harry Potter *series. Far from harming young readers, these books have encouraged more children to read. Perhaps the principal quandary pertaining to book banning is that it often has the opposite effect intended: many readers purposely seek out banned material.*

More and more teachers are looking over their shoulders during read-aloud or SSR [Sustained Silent Reading] periods, worrying that someone in the community will take offense at some book. The frequency of such fears sometimes makes me wonder whether this is America or Iraq. In our free and constitutional society, everyone has right to protest anything—something many citizens in other countries can't boast.

Protesters have a right to protest and a right to be heard. What they *don't* have is the right to impose *their* will on *others*. In a nation governed by "majority rules," they have only the right to persuade the majority toward their point of view.

There is a natural instinct in parents to protect their young. Since there is not always universal agreement on what hurts and what helps children, conflicts arise. A book that might be appropriate for ninth-graders might be very inappropriate for third-graders. Doesn't a parent have a right, if not an obligation, to speak out on such an occasion? And that's why districts should have clearly defined censorship policies in place, defining a board to hear the complaint, read the offending book, and make a decision on its appropriateness.

I recall two recent complaints given to me at seminars: A mother arguing that *Gone With the Wind* should not be included in a fourth-grade classroom and another who urged that *Snow Falling on Cedars* should not be made part of the eighth-grade core curriculum. I agreed with both parties, not from a moral standpoint but from a curriculum standpoint. Both books were written with adult audiences in mind, including a writing structure, historic perspective, and subject matter that are not within the normal range of development for children in those respective grades.

There is also the problem of an elementary school buying a prelabeled and prepackaged book collection for use with programs like Accelerated Reader, only to find an irate parent complaining that a certain book with predetermined fifth-grade reading level contains subject matter that is more appropriate for middle or high school students. . . .

It has been made more than obvious that exposing children to the classics before they can handle them has NOT resulted in either higher reading scores or higher sales for classics, so why would someone think these two adult novels will do that? There's more than enough room for these books in the home or the school/public library. (The eighth-grade *Cedars* choice smacks of secondary teachers who personally prefer reading "adult" over "young adult" literature and probably would opt to teach on the college level anyway.)

Jonathan Zimmerman, a New York University professor of education history, explored the history of censorship in the classroom in his essay, "Harry Potter and His Censors," in *Education Week*, Aug. 2, 2000. Though an ardent fan of the *Potter* series, Zimmerman cautions against knee-jerk reactions to all censor-groups, based upon the valid claims of other groups throughout the history of the American classroom. His citations of "Little Black Sambo" and anti-semitic stories in New York City textbooks as recently as the 1950s should give everyone pause for thought.

If the *Potter* books had included racist or anti-Catholic language, many of Potter's most ardent defenders would be switching sides. If that's not "selective" censorship, it is at least worth considering before condemning every book complaint.

Even the most liberal of artists must concede the incivility of uncensored speech or behavior. Author and entertainer Steve Allen was a powerful advocate for "appropriate" censorship within the television industry as it grew increasingly violent and vulgar during the 80's and 90's. As honorary chairman of the Parents Television Council, he built a reasoned argument for monitoring and censoring (if necessary), whatever was brought before the eyes of children.

As a confirmed liberal, author of more than 60 books and 1000 songs, and creator of some of television's most entertaining and cerebral moments, even Allen conceded that everything is not appropriate for the young. . . .

The Battle Over Harry Potter

Conceding Prof. Zimmerman's and Steve Allen's very valid points, I must also note that a democracy like ours hatches an inordinate number of religious and political fanatics. Anything new, popular, or magical becomes the "anti-Christ," as Rev. Jerry Falwell demonstrated with the Teletubbies.

Considering how long parents, teachers, and librarians prayed for children to turn off the TV, drop the Game Boy, discard the Walkman, unhook the cell phone, walk away from the mall, and start reading, it's perplexing that when it finally happened—and happened big time with 400- to 700-page books that were thicker than most classics, the critics didn't drop to their knees and thank the Lord for answering their prayers. Instead, they declared the devil was behind it. Strange. It reminded me of those who predicted Y2K would be *Armageddon*. I didn't mind them thinking that, but I'd sure object to them forcing me into their bomb shelter—which is what censors often try to do.

The furor over the *Potter* books is not dissimilar to one in J. K. Rowling's adopted Scottish homeland in 1847 when Sir James Young Simpson dared to introduce pain-killing anesthetics to the maternity ward. Church leaders immediately accused him of circumventing God's will ("If God imposes pain in childbirth, who is man to nullify it?"). Today, of course, Simpson's practices are commonly used in both Christian and secular hospitals throughout the world.

The *Potter* books topped the 1999 top-ten list of protested books compiled annually by American Library Association's Office for Intellectual Freedom with 472 complaints about the books' focus on wizardry and magic. Nonetheless few communities found any merit for banning the works. Indeed, evangelical Christian radio talk show host Charles Colson gave the books a very "positive" review, calling them "enormously inventive," and assured parent-listeners that Harry's magic is "mechanical as opposed to occultic." Struggling with good and evil forces, Harry and his friends do not "make contact with a supernatural world."

Like the majority of people, I believe the *Potter* books are written in broad-stroke farce/fun. They won't turn children into the devil's disciples but will go a long way toward turning them into rabid readers. If we wrote textbooks like this, students would be *volunteering* for homework. And if we're going to ban "witch" books, the first to go would be, sadly, the Christian allegory *The Lion, the Witch, and the Wardrobe* by C. S. Lewis.... It's only a short hop from thinking Harry is doing the devil's work to thinking that Harry's poor dead parents were really Julius and Ethel Rosenberg [the Rosenbergs were accused of being communist spies during the 1950s. They were tried and executed for their crimes.].

Seldom is a book successfully banned but sales and circulation always increase as a result of the attempt.

The Popularity of Forbidden Books

John Monk, an editorial writer for Knight-Ridder's *The State* in Columbia, South Carolina, wrote an editorial in response to the protests, noting: "Some claim the *Potter* books lure children into witchcraft. Poppycock. You might as well say *Gone With the Wind* teaches young readers to be slave owners, or *Treasure Island* entices children to be pirates, or *Peter Pan* urges children to run away from home."

In February, 2003, the Vatican made an official statement regarding Harry Potter's magic relationship with children. Rev. Don Peter Fleetwood, a Vatican culture official, stated that he saw no problems with the magic embraced in the Potter books. "If I have understood well the intentions of Harry Potter's author, they [magic forces] help children to see the difference between good and evil." ...

The book-banners might also consider the concept of "forbidden fruit" and its effect on human behavior. Seldom is a book successfully banned but sales and circulation always increase as a result of the attempt. Book bannings make as much sense as a parent telling her children in December,

"Don't look in the back of the hall closet." You've just advertised the fact that something is there you don't want them to see. This is true for both children and adults.

The adult reaction is exemplified in the story told to me by Nancy Weatherman of the Tennessee State Library and Archives. She had successfully weeded an antiquated library collection in one of the state's prisons when the warden wanted to know how she planned to dispose of the hundreds of books she'd weeded.

"That's easy," she told him. "Just pile them on tables under a sign 'Do Not Touch!' They'll be gone in days." They were.

Children's reactions are much the same. When Michael Dirda, editor of the *Washington Post's Book World* declared the film *Jurassic Park* to be too frightening and therefore off-limits to his nine-year-old son, he failed to take into consideration the lure of "forbidden fruit." That attraction, combined with the television commercials, were enough to provoke the boy to go to the original source. Painstakingly but with great motivation, the nine-year-old read the entire 399-page book that summer. This, in turn, provoked the father-editor to wonder if maybe this isn't the key to turning on all those reluctant readers: *Make movies of our great books, and then forbid children to see them.*

6

Book Banning Protects Family Values

Rebecca Hagelin

Rebecca Hagelin is the author of Home Invasion: Protecting Your Family in a Culture That's Gone Stark Raving Mad *and a vice president of communications and marketing at the Heritage Foundation.*

While we as a society have been taught to believe that any reading is good for adolescents, it is important to consider the kinds of books that children are reading. The American Library Association (ALA), for instance, recommends books for young readers, but these recommendations reflect the organization's liberal values. Books recommended by the ALA contain curse words and graphic sexual information. In order to guarantee that a child is reading quality books—books that a parent approves of—a parent should review a child's reading material beforehand. It is a parent's responsibility—not the ALA's and not an educational institution's—to decide what a child should read.

Reading isn't always good for our kids.

How's that for an opening sentence to stir a little controversy among the educational elites?

We've been bombarded by so many messages about how reading expands the mind, excites the imagination and enhances the vocabulary (all of which are true) that many par-

Rebecca Hagelin, "Are Your Kids Reading Rot?", *Townhall*, August 16, 2005. Reproduced by permission. www.townhall.com

ents have forgotten that the benefit of reading for our children very much depends on what they're reading. And, I'm afraid that many children spend hours reading what often turns out to be pure rot.

With school starting all over the country between last week and just after Labor Day, it's time for a reading warning: Parents, beware.

In many cases the very liberal American Library Association exerts great influence over what reading materials teachers assign their students. But that material may be highly inappropriate for your child. Don't let the following scenario unfold in your home:

Mrs. Jones hands out a book report assignment that includes several books for her class to choose from. Mom dutifully drives Suzi to the local library and browses while Suzi selects her book. Within half an hour, book in hand, everyone is feeling rather satisfied that they have been so responsible in starting on the project early. Mom and Suzi arrive home, and while mom begins making dinner, the conscientious and responsible Suzi heads to her room and begins to consume what turns out to be highly sexualized, vulgar garbage, filled with four-letter words and enough verbal porn to embarrass even an ol' salt.

Mom doesn't have a clue that her daughter's innocence has just been molested in the privacy of her own bedroom. She won't ever know because Suzi, a bit stymied by the fact that Mom took her to get a book that her teacher assigned, will be too embarrassed and confused to ever tell. Yet, she's just had sexuality, relationships and acceptable behavior defined for her by some perverted author most folks have never heard of. And the kid was simply trying to get her homework done.

Inappropriate Books for Young Readers

While researching my book, *Home Invasion: Protecting Your Family in a Culture That's Gone Stark Raving Mad*, I took an

ALA-recommended reading list for 13- and 14-year-olds to my local library and headed to the "Young Adult" section (code for "pre-teen" and "teen"). I found some books from the list; others were already checked out. One book, the librarian told me, had just been returned, but hadn't been re-shelved, so I patiently waited while she went into the back room to retrieve it.

With several items in hand, I headed back to the Young Adult section, where I couldn't help but notice pre-teen and teen girls and guys in various stages of development and maturity, dutifully searching the shelves for assigned books. I sat down on a reading bench and began flipping through the pages of the book that had just been returned.

There's something very moving about holding a book in your hand that a child has just finished reading. But the warmth in my heart soon turned into a sickening feeling in my gut when I began to read passages so cheap and trashy that I could scarcely believe my eyes. I only had to get to page four before the first of many uses of the term "motherf—" showed up. Several scenes described, in graphic detail, sexual acts between teenagers.

In the interest of decency, there's no way I can give you word-for-word examples. And I refuse to give the trashy book and its loser author free publicity in a column that often gets forwarded around the World Wide Web. I'd rather parents and other adults who care about our children and their education—and whether . . . educational elites indoctrinate them in immorality—actually go to their local library and research the reading lists themselves.

Lest you think the first book was put on the list in error, the next recommended teen item I thumbed through was equally as nauseating. A sexual act between fourth-graders was a "highlight," as well as graphic details of sex between teens, including a homosexual encounter. And this is the garbage that today's educators pass off as great literature for our children? The great classics, meanwhile, are all but missing. One list I reviewed for eight-graders contained about 20 authors—none recognizable save the lone great Mark Twain. And they call this education?

The lesson here is simple. Moms and dads: Don't just naively drive your kids to the library—you must be careful to help them choose books that reflect your values. Even if your kids are in private school, you're hardly safe—many of the best schools blindly use ALA lists. Of course, if you home school your kids, you're probably already aware of the moral problems of many ALA decisions, but even if you're using a good curriculum guide, it's always best to preview the books first.

The ALA is quick to call anyone who questions its decisions a "censor." But remember, part of our responsibility and privilege as parents is to be the ones who determine what is and is not appropriate for our own children.

7

Book Banning Handicaps the Educational Process

Diane Ravitch

Diane Ravitch served as U.S. Assistant Secretary of Education from 1991 through 1993 and is a professor of education at New York University. She is an acclaimed education historian and the author of seven books.

Because materials used in schools have been heavily censored to protect adolescents from many kinds of information, homogenized textbooks cannot compete with the excitement of popular media (music, television, and the Internet). Under the current system, schools are restrained from offering students the compelling stories of history. Literature should do more than comfort young readers; literature should teach young readers to better understand the world they live in. Handicapping the educational system through censorship may have long-term consequences in how we communicate as a society. By failing to provide the raw materials students need to understand our common culture, American education is undermining one of the country's original precepts—"we the people."

Think about the strange contradiction in the life of a high school student today. At home, she watches television and sees news about terrorism, hijackings, massacres, famines, and political upheavals. She goes on-line, where the Internet gives her access to anything and everything. She goes to the movies, where she enters a world of fantasy, romance, passion, excitement, and action. She listens to music and hears the latest hip-hop, rap, or heavy metal performers. Before she falls asleep at night, she e-mails gossip to her friends.

Monday through Friday, she goes to school. There she will open her literature textbook to a story that has been carefully chosen for its inoffensive language. The teacher points out that the story was written by a woman; the student doesn't care. It's boring. She will read entries written by students her age. She will quickly skip over all the pedagogical junk about critical thinking, looking for something interesting. She won't find it. Then she moves to history class, where the class is studying the role of women in the Revolutionary War; the text says that twenty thousand women fought in the war. Really? Hmmm. Yawn.

Schools cannot beat the entertainment industry at its own game.

Little, maybe nothing that happens in the classroom can compete with the powerful stimuli that she can easily find on television, in the movies, on her CDs, in video games, and on the Internet. For her and her friends, school is the Empire of Boredom. They do not know and surely do not care that an entire industry of bias reviewers has insulated them from any contact in their textbooks with anything that might disturb them, like violence, death, divorce, or bad language. They are safe, but they are bored.

No matter. When the school day is done, they will turn again to the videos and music and movies that feed them eroticized violence and surround them with language that knows no constraints. This is as wacky a combination as anyone might dream up: schools in which life has been homogenized, with all conflicts flattened out, within the context of an adolescent culture in which anything goes.

Schools cannot beat the entertainment industry at its own game. What they have to offer students is the chance for intellectual freedom, the power to think for themselves rather than gorge themselves on the media's steady diet of junk food.

But under the present regime of censorship, the schools themselves are not intellectually free. They cannot awaken young people's minds with great literature when the stuff in their literature textbooks is so banal, so ordinary, so engineered to appeal to childish narcissism. They cannot expect students to think critically about social issues and the world when their history textbooks do not demonstrate critical thinking. When their reading is constrained by the fine filter of bias and sensitivity codes, how can it possibly contribute to the forming of critical and independent minds? How can young people discover the drama of history when their textbooks anesthetize them with a relentless slog across the centuries, lumbering from one event to the next, from one culture to the next? Great history consists of great stories, surprising convergences, the conflict of powerful ideas, and the historian's insights into motivation and character that illuminate the life of a man or woman—but all of that has been sacrificed to the gods of coverage and cultural equivalence.

Great literature does not comfort us; it does not make us feel better about ourselves.

The Power of Literature and History

Something is terribly wrong here. The schools should be the great agencies of social and intellectual equality. This they cannot be unless they can give all children access to great literature and teach them the joy of reading. Reading is the key to future success; it builds vocabulary, it enriches the imagination, it opens new worlds. The novelist Mario Vargas Llosa has argued that new technologies will not replace literature. The new technologies are fast, and they are exciting, but they are only a means of getting information. What literature offers is a common denominator for understanding human experience; it allows human beings to recognize one another across time and space. By reading great literature, Vargas Llosa argues, we learn "what remains common in all of us under the broad range of differences that separates us. Nothing better protects a human being against the stupidity of prejudice, racism, religious or political sectarianism, and exclusivist nationalism than this truth that invariably appears in great literature: that men and women of all nations and places are essentially equal, and that only injustice sows among them discrimination, fear, and exploitation." Literature, in other words, actually does what the bias and sensitivity codes claim to do: It teaches us about our common humanity. And it does so by speaking candidly to our souls, not by censoring what we read.

Great literature does not comfort us; it does not make us feel better about ourselves. It is not written to enhance our self-esteem or to make us feel that we are "included" in the story. It takes us into its own world and creates its own reality. It shakes us up; it makes us think. Sometimes it makes us cry.

The same is true of the study of history. It is possible to spend one's time learning only about one's own family or ethnic group. But there are worlds of adventure, worlds of tragedy awaiting us if we are willing to let go of our solipsism, our narcissism, our need to study only ourselves.

The flight from knowledge and content in the past generation has harmed our children and diminished our culture. As they advance in school, children recognize that what they see on television is far more realistic and thought-provoking than the sanitized world of their textbooks. The numbing nihilism of the contentless curriculum produced by the puritans of left and right merely feeds the appetite for the exciting nihilism of an uncensored and sensationalized popular culture, skillfully produced by amoral entrepreneurs who are expert at targeting the tastes of bored teenagers.

We do not know how these trends may yet affect the quality of our politics, our civic life, and our ability to communicate with one another somewhere above the level of the lowest common denominator. The consequences can't be good. As the technologies of the entertainment industry become more sophisticated, so too will its appeals to emotion, to feelings, to our basest instincts.

When we as a nation set out to provide universal access to education, our hope was that intelligence and reason would one day prevail and make a better world where issues would be resolved by thoughtful deliberation. The great goal of education was not to cultivate an elite, but to abolish class distinctions to the extent that education can do so. Here is the rub. Intelligence and reason cannot be achieved merely by skill-building and immersion in new technologies; elites have always known this and have always insisted on more for their children. Intelligence and reason cannot be developed absent the judgment that is formed by prolonged and thoughtful study of history, literature, and culture, not only that of our own nation, but of other civilizations as well.

That is not what our children get today. Instead, they get faux literature, and they get history that lightly skims across the surface of events, with no time to become engaged in ideas or to delve beneath the surface. Not only does censorship diminish the intellectual vitality of the curriculum, it also erodes our commitment to a common culture. It demands that we abandon our belief in *e pluribus unum* [one from many], a diverse people who are continually becoming one. The common culture is not static; it evolves to reflect the people we are becoming. But even as it changes, it preserves the memory of "we, the people" in song and story; whatever our origins, we too become part of the American story, neither its first nor its last chapter. We are not strangers, and we do not begin our national life anew in every generation. Our nation has a history and a literature, to which we contribute.

We must build on that common culture, not demolish it. As our common culture grows stronger, as we make it stronger, so too grows our recognition that we share a common destiny.

8

Individuals Should Make Their Own Decisions about Censored Books

Val Ross

Val Ross is a journalist and winner of the National Newspaper Award.

As the Christian church in Iceland attempted to uproot older Pagan beliefs, legends circulated about the power of the old books that had been written by sorcerers. In one legend, three boys traveled to a graveyard where an old man leading a cow on a rope handed one of the boys—Eirikur—a book. Eirikur remained awake all night reading the book, but stopped before he reached the last page: he feared that if he read any further he would lose his soul to the devil. While Norse legends may seem unrelated to present times, many people continue to fear the power of books. Despite the harmless nature of Harry Potter and the Sorcerer's Stone, *the book has often been challenged in the United States and Canada. The power of books cannot be denied and individuals have a responsibility to decide when they should stop reading a book.*

On a long summer day around the year 1620, three boys—Big Magnus, Little Bogi, and their friend Eirikur, the cleverest, bravest boy in all Iceland—went searching for a book of magic. In those days, most boys their age in mainland Europe could not even read, but in Iceland, isolated in the midst of the North Atlantic, learning and writing were prized. On long winter nights, when the darkness closed in and the sheep huddled in the barns and the fishing boats stayed in port, there wasn't much to do but sit with a book by the fire.

Iceland became Christian in the year 1030, but for years it had a kind of Christianity that would have shocked people in mainland Europe. Icelanders tolerated people who kept alive the old pagan ways, who made herbal potions or chanted spells calling on the power of the Norse gods. By 1600 the Church got more strict about these pagan remnants, and possessing a book of sorcery was punishable by death. Yet even church leaders themselves were curious about those old ways.

In Iceland, summer night skies stay light, so Bogi, Magnus, and Eirikur weren't worried about darkness overtaking them as they set off across the hilly meadows. They were determined to find the magic book *Raudskinna—Redskin—*said to have been buried along with its owner, a strange old man who had lived alone with his cow, and who might have practiced the ancient ways.

"I've heard this book *Raudskinna* was written at the Black School," Eirikur told his friends.

"What was the Black School?"

"A place where wizards studied long ago," Eirikur replied over his shoulder. "There were no teachers . . . the students just said what they wanted to learn, and then they would enter a dark room, or maybe a cave. It was so dark they couldn't see anything—until books appeared, written in fiery red letters. The students had no other light, just letters lit from within."

Bogi the curious asked, "Reading in the darkness?"

Big Magnus pushed him violently. "You fool! They were magicians!"

But Eirikur had another explanation. "Everyone who is ignorant reads in darkness. Then they become . . . enlightened."

At last Eirikur stopped by the entrance to an old church-yard. The tombstones cast long shadows in the mauve evening light. Bogi shuddered, and Magnus said softly, "Maybe we should not be looking for this book."

Even in our own time, some people fear that books about magic really have some unhealthy power.

But Eirikur was full of daring. "What if the book is real?" he said. "What if it has power, knowledge that we can use to do good—find lost sheep, foretell storms, stop fishermen from getting drowned at sea . . . ?" Pushing on into the churchyard, he scanned the tombstones, looking for the hermit's grave.

Suddenly Magnus cried out. Someone was approaching: a stranger with hollow eyes, leading a cow on a rope. Under his arm was a huge book bound in red leather.

"!" breathed Eirikur.

"Here," said the old man, with a strange smile. Giving Eirikur the book, he melted away into the deepening shadows.

The boys wrapped themselves in cloaks of animal skins and tried to keep warm as Eirikur read in the twilit northern night, page by page.

Finally the sky began to brighten again. "Morning?" asked Bogi, shivering.

Eirikur looked up. He was just coming to the last pages. He slammed the book shut and looked around.

The old man had come back. He was smiling.

Eirikur thrust the red-covered book at him. "Take it!" he cried.

The old man's smile dropped away. He looked shocked, as if Eirikur had denied him some prize. Furiously he tucked away the old book. Then he seemed to vanish.

Eirikur was very quiet, and he let Big Magnus lead the way home. The three boys walked in silence. Finally Bogi could no longer help himself. "What did you read?" he blurted.

"Just enough," Eirikur told him. "Enough to know that if I had read any further, I would have lost my soul to the Devil."

The Power of Books

There are many versions of the story of the magic book *Raudskinna* and Eirikur, a real person who lived in the 1600s and later became a famous Christian bishop. What really happened in Eirikur's search for knowledge, we have no way of knowing. But the legend of *Raudskinna* is not only a version of the struggle between Iceland's old religion and the new; it is also a way of telling of each reader's struggle to judge whether the contents of a book are evil or useful.

[T]he censors are right to respect the power of books, and to remind us all that books contain forces we may not fully appreciate.

This struggle has gone on since the dawn of the written word. In 1559, just before the time of Eirikur, the Vatican issued its *Index Librorum Prohibitorum*, the Catholic Church's official list of forbidden books. On the list were Martin Luther and William Tyndale, and books thought to contain magic. One, *The Book of Secrets of Albertus Magnus*, was actually just a collection of herbal remedies compiled by a helpful monk around 1250. But by 1605 those herbal remedies looked like satanic potions, and *The Book of Secrets* went on the index.

Even in our own time, some people fear that books about magic really have some unhealthy power. J. K. Rowling's story of a student wizard, *Harry Potter and the Philosopher's Stone* [titled *Harry Potter and the Sorceror's Stone* in the United States], has had the weird distinction of being the most challenged book in library and public school collections in the United States. In Canada, after an uproar at the Durham Region School Board near Toronto, school officials sent home consent forms for parents to sign before their children could open a copy of *Harry Potter*.

We should take the censors seriously. Of course, they are wrong to fear Harry Potter, who, after all, is a good person who stands by his friends and tries to defeat evil. But the censors are right to respect the power of books, and to remind us all that books contain forces we may not fully appreciate. Ultimately, though, each reader—like young Eirikur—has a responsibility to know when to shut the covers.

9

Book Banning Endangers Majority Values

Linda Harvey

Linda Harvey is the president of Mission America, a pro-family organization that monitors homosexual activism in youth culture.

Banned Books Week presents itself as a yearly event that supports First Amendment rights. In reality, Banned Books Week fails to recognize a form of censorship that occurs frequently in libraries: the censoring of books with conservative points of view. This has been especially true concerning books about homosexuality aimed at young readers. Libraries carry many items espousing a liberal political point of view and very few espousing a conservative one. Libraries hide information about gay-themed books from parents and ignore the fact that many gay-themed books contain inaccurate information. The only way for parents to correct the current situation is to remind librarians that taxpayers support them.

Libraries and schools throughout the country are ready once again to observe Banned Books Week. It's that special time each year when some in the library profession point an accusing finger at parents, especially Christians or conservatives who might dare to question the value or appropriateness of certain materials available to youth. For 25 years since its inception, Banned Books Week has been warning America: "Beware of the ignorance and repression of censors! They will deprive us all of valuable knowledge and freedom."

Linda Harvey, "Banned Books Week: Smoke Screen of Hypocrisy," *World Net Daily*, September 23, 2005. Reproduced by permission. www.worldnetdaily.com.

Setting aside any danger that the government might ban valuable materials, which is not happening in any community in America, let's strip away the spin and look at the facts. The supposed dangers are essentially phony. For there are several methods to "ban" a book from a school or library: someone can ask that something already in the library be removed, or, valuable books can be banned from consideration before they ever reach the shelves. This is the dirty little secret behind the bluster and outrage of Banned Books Week: private, library-initiated censorship is a routine practice throughout America.

Library selection committees are systematically purging libraries of any conservative or serious Christian viewpoints and instead, loading the shelves with left-wing propaganda and pornography. This year, the American Library Association [ALA] is making a special to-do about the "dangers" of objections to "gay-themed books" especially those for youth. While it's doubtful this is an issue that keeps most Americans awake at night, it's important to recognize that as controversial social issues go, there is hardly a more hot-button topic, and one would think that all these "free-speech" advocates and defenders of philosophical liberties would be worried about any suppression of viewpoints on this high-profile subject. Don't the vigilant watchdogs of tolerance seek to protect a "diversity" of thought?

There's no doubt that any curious child or teen will be able to find ample reading material at the library, all presenting only one admiring side of the issue, sometimes quite graphically.

An Unbalanced Library Collection

Well, the microcosm of my local library in a suburb of Columbus, Ohio, reflects what many are reporting from around the nation: Conservative materials on the issue of homosexuality are disappearing from the collection, or more often, never appearing in the first place. In researching the catalog of the Upper Arlington Public Library, I searched under titles, authors and subjects for books providing a responsible defense of traditional marriage and warning about the risks of homosexual behavior.

I searched under "homosexuality," "gay and lesbian," "traditional marriage," "Christian morality," "ex-gay," "ex-homosexual," and many other phrases. My search yielded four non-fiction books expressing a conservative viewpoint.

But of books, DVDs and videos offering a pro-homosexual view, the smorgasbord is overflowing. There are guides to "gay and lesbian" rights from the American Civil Liberties Union and others. There are books about affirming one's "gay" children authored by Betty De Generes as well as those with less-stellar offspring. There are books by columnists and activists: Andrew Sullivan, Pat Califia, Kevin Jennings, Evan Wolfson, and Candace Gingrich. There is the pro-homosexual view of the Bible—*What the Bible Really Says About Homosexuality*—and of course, Mel White, the defender of homosexuals from the "spiritual violence" of Bible-believing Christians.

And time doesn't even permit me to cover all the many offerings detailing homosexual, bisexual and group sex, nor the selections arguing for more tolerance and understanding of adults having sex with children—"intergenerational intimacy" is the new name for pedophilia.

In the section of the library aimed toward adults, I stopped counting at 100 pro-homosexual books.

Gay-Themed Books for Children and Teens

And for children and teens? With at least 70 offerings, mostly within the recent genre of "gay teen fiction," the young people in our community are set. There's no doubt that any curious child or teen will be able to find ample reading material at the library, all presenting only one admiring side of the issue, sometimes quite graphically.

There are explicit titles kids may need to conceal from parental eyes, such as *Boy Meets Boy* and *Kissing Kate*. For the gender-questioning crowd, there's *A Boy Named Phyllis* or for smaller kids, *Oliver Button is a Sissy*. There's the quite graphic novel, *The Perks of Being a Wallflower*, which, according to the ALA, was one of the most challenged books in 2004. And for non-fiction, teens are somehow supposed to benefit from reading books like *In Your Face: Stories from the Lives of Queer Youth*, a book revealing the depressing, chaotic backgrounds of homosexually-attracted youth. In the thoughtful reader, it provokes obvious cause-effect questions that, like the elephant in the room, the book ignores.

Then, belying anti-bigotry ideals, teens can be indoctrinated by either a print version, a DVD or a video of the play and film *The Laramie Project*, presenting an inaccurate and distorted account of the Matthew Shepard case, including the requisite portrayal of rabid fundamentalists, the kind the left needs to believe caused Shepard's death. This category includes, of course, all conservatives.

Little children can choose the infamous *Heather Has Two Mommies* or *And Tango Makes Three*, which is supposed to teach children the valuable lesson that if two male penguins in Central Park Zoo can pair up and adopt a baby penguin, same-sex coupling must be OK for humans, too. Only problem is that the real penguin duo inspiring this story has split. Silo recently discovered his male attraction to a female penguin, blasting the interspecies analogy to bits. Yet the misleading book remains.

When will library-instigated book banning come out of the closet?

The ALA is terribly concerned that these "gay-themed" books be available for our youth. After all, their standards, adopted by many libraries in this country, urge librarians to "model and promote a non-judgmental attitude toward . . . and preserve confidentiality in interactions with young adults." This has a nice ring until one learns three things: the ALA defines "young adults" as ages 12 to 20—they recommend that no item in a library be off-limits to a child at any age who requests it. *Therefore, the obvious meaning of "confidentiality" is that they have a goal of withholding information from parents.*

Is there hope that more librarians can come to understand the harmful nature of sexually graphic, violent and dark depressing materials in the hands of our children? That homosexuality is a life-shortening road down which no responsible adult should point any child? That, if they refuse to recognize the fallacy of a pro-homosexual viewpoint, then at the very least, every child, every person who accesses libraries in America should have the option of access to both sides of this issue?

When will library-instigated book banning come out of the closet? Not until we, parents and citizens, make specific requests to add thoughtful pro-family books to balance these collections, if we can't have the inaccurate and high-risk material removed. We need to also, as a conservative movement, encourage publishers to print more books dealing with this issue, especially for young people.

It's time for us taxpayers to remind librarians, for those who've forgotten, that they report to us.

10

Book Banning Protects Minority Values

Irene Monroe

The Reverend Irene Monroe is author of the column "Queer Take" for The Witness.

Many books for young readers that focus on gay themes have proven controversial, leading the religious right to challenge and attempt to ban them. Libraries, however, have always served as open institutions, representing views from different cultures and peoples. When books are taken off the library shelf for promoting lesbian, gay, bisexual, transgender, and queer people's points of view, society becomes less tolerant; when these books remain on library shelves, young readers are encouraged to understand and respect other lifestyles. By encouraging tolerance, books can help make young readers better people.

Banning books is not a new idea, but it is the latest chapter in the culture war against lesbian, gay, bisexual, transgender and queer [LGBTQ] people. While anti-gay children's literature is a mainstay in conservative school districts and libraries across the country, LGBTQ-friendly children's books are not. And in the war concerning "moral values," religious conservatives righteously feel they must do all they can to stop the distribution of LGBTQ-friendly children's books before they leave the publisher's desk.

At the annual Book Expo America held earlier this month [June 2005] in New York, publishers displayed new books

Irene Monroe, "Book Banning Is Not a Moral Value," *Witness Magazine*, June 28, 2005. Reproduced by permission. www.thewitness.org.

about LGBTQ people written for children. One of Book Expo America's most controversial children's books was *King & King*, about a prince who falls in love with another prince.

"It's inclusive. This is a book that librarians can recommend to parents because there isn't another book like it. It's a very positive book about gay people. Anyway, it's widely purchased by libraries, and it's in most libraries," said Phil Wood, publisher of San Francisco's Ten Speed Press, which published *King & King*, to ABC News.

However, in some libraries and school districts, *King & King* will not see the light of day because it is believed to be robbing children of their innocence and promoting sodomy and pedophilia.

"When a book of a very bizarre nature, a very offensive nature, is found in a library in an area that would be considered very conservative, this tends to raise some eyebrows. It certainly goes against our family values that we so treasure here in Louisiana," Republican state Rep. A. G. Crowe told ABC News.

Libraries are a gateway to the world. They open our minds.

Because of the outrage concerning *King & King*, Crowe wrote a resolution to urge librarians to keep books with LGBTQ content away from school kids.

Books Open Minds

In writing about this subject, I am reminded of my childhood favorite, Ray Bradbury's sci-fi novel *Fahrenheit 451*. It's about book-burning and censorship in a futuristic American city. Bradbury illustrates that the salient factor leading to censorship is the objections of special-interest groups. In *Fahrenheit 451*, authors attempt to write books that do not offend anyone or create any conflicting opinions. However, the city decides that the only way to avoid objectionable content is to simply burn all the books. If Bradbury were writing his classic today, the special-interest group in question would be religious conservatives.

Libraries are a gateway to the world. They open our minds. One of the places we can gradually begin to see attempts toward American democracy is in America's classrooms and libraries. Our classrooms and libraries have the greatest potential to open us all to a wonderful world of different people and cultures. Our libraries are places that we can not only learn about different people and cultures, but we can also have them up close in our classrooms. And in so doing, we not only open ourselves up to ethnically and culturally different students sitting and living among us, but we also open ourselves up to ethically and culturally different people of the world.

Banning books that religious conservatives deem as objectionable, however, creates a moralistic view of LGBTQ people that engenders a cult-like mentality, instills fear, robs society of its rich diversity, and interferes with school policies to create an environment that is safe for all children.

Banning books also prohibits an individual from thinking freely. In *Fahrenheit 451*, a character depicts what it's like to rob the mind of knowledge. "We must all be alike. Not everyone born free and equal, as the constitution says. . . . A book is a loaded gun. . . . Burn it. Take the shot from the weapon. Breach man's mind."

We should all want to be part of creating a safe and welcoming world for our children.

Books Teach Tolerance

There is a tremendous cost to us as a society in banning books with LGBTQ-friendly themes because it increases intolerance and insensitivity, and it ignores our plight for civil rights.

"I think the important part is for a kid to see himself in a book, and equally important for a kid to see people who are not like themselves in books, so they can learn to be tolerant of people who are not like them," David Gale, vice president and editorial director of Simon & Schuster Books for Young Readers, told ABC News.

The key word here is tolerant, and in making our schools and society safe for our children it is important to teach them to be tolerant of people not like themselves. I am reminded of Dorothy Law Nolte's poem "Children Learn What They Live," in which she wrote:

If children live with criticism, they
learn to condemn.

If children live with hostility, they
learn to fight.

If children live with ridicule, they
learn to be shy.

If children live with shame, they
learn to feel guilty.

If children live with tolerance, they
learn to be patient.

If children live with encouragement, they learn confidence.

If children live with praise, they
learn to appreciate.

If children live with fairness, they
learn justice.

If children live with security, they
learn to have faith.

If children live with approval, they
learn to like themselves.

If children live with acceptance and
friendship, they learn to find love
in the world.

We should all want to be part of creating a safe and welcoming world for our children. Outside of the home environment, schools and libraries must be the next place. Most educators today know that, especially those trying to meet today's educational and cultural challenges. Educators have an obligation to develop a safe environment and multicultural curriculum that includes the history, culture and experiences of LGBTQ people.

In so doing, we will make all of our children better doctors, better lawyers, better teachers, better neighbors, and better human beings—creating a stronger nation and finer world in which to live.

11

Banned Books Teach Tolerance

Kathie Durbin

Kathie Durbin is a journalist and author of Tree Huggers: Victory, Defeat & Renewal in the Northwest Ancient Forest Campaign.

Book banning is an American tradition, and it has been increasingly common for classic literature to be challenged and banned from school systems. Books are challenged for multiple reasons and even the process of challenging a book creates acrimony between teachers, school boards, and a community. While many teachers believe that young adults are capable of comprehending controversial materials, parents and the community frequently object. While the Supreme Court has ruled that school boards have discretion when deciding which books will be available in school libraries, the court also ruled that school boards must consider community standards. Challenges and bans, however, are robbing teachers of valuable tools and children of literature that represents the world they live in.

Eleanor Cumberland recalls vividly the school desegregation wars that erupted in the farming community of Hillsboro, Ohio, a half-century ago.

In 1954, the year she entered 7th grade, her mother, Imogene Curtis, helped mobilize a campaign of daily marches by black students to whites-only schools. Turned away at the schoolhouse door, Curtis and other black parents home-

Kathie Durbin, "Books Under Fire," *Teaching Tolerance*, vol. 27, Spring 2005. Reproduced by permission. www.tolerance.org.

schooled their children and, with help from the NAACP [National Association for the Advancement of Colored People], brought the first civil rights lawsuit in the North under the U.S. Supreme Court's 1954 *Brown v. Board of Education* ruling. Eleanor Cumberland's house was used as a makeshift school during the protracted legal battle.

So it was with full awareness of the history of the civil rights struggle that the 63-year-old retired nurse's aide in 2004 asked Hillsboro High Principal Larry Stall to remove Harper Lee's *To Kill a Mockingbird* from the 9th-grade English curriculum.

The critically acclaimed novel, set in the fictional Alabama community of Maycomb during the Great Depression, tells the story of a town torn by the trial of a black man wrongly accused of raping a white woman; of Atticus Finch, the white lawyer who defends him; and of his children, Jem and Scout, through whose voices the events unfold.

Notwithstanding the First Amendment, book banning is a practice rooted in American history.

To Kill a Mockingbird consistently ranks near the top of the American Library Association's [ALA] list of 100 most frequently banned books. Most complaints involve the use of language now considered racially offensive, including the N–word.

"I feel the book serves no purpose but to keep racism and separatism alive in a day when we're supposed to be teaching love and equality," Cumberland said in a letter to the principal. "In all reality, we know these feelings of hatred and prejudice are still harbored by some people, but should those responsible for our children's education play a part in keeping bigotry, superiority and hatred alive?"

"*To Kill a Mockingbird* is a work of art that clearly confronts racism," Superintendent Byron Wisecup responded.

"The highest result of education is teaching tolerance. This book is unflinching in its condemnation of racial prejudice."

At the recommendation of a review committee, he kept the book in the curriculum.

Mockingbird is in good company. Mark Twain's *Adventures of Huckleberry Finn*, J. D. Salinger's *The Catcher in the Rye* and J. K. Rowling's wildly popular *Harry Potter* series routinely make the ALA's list of most-challenged books.

Book Banning is Rooted in History

Notwithstanding the First Amendment, book banning is a practice rooted in American history. In 1873, Congress passed the Comstock Law in an effort to legislate public morality. Though rarely enforced, the act remains on the books.

A survey by the National School Boards Association found that one-third of challenges to school reading materials in the 1990s resulted in the withdrawal or restriction of those materials.

Whatever the motive, efforts to restrict access to books deemed objectionable can polarize communities, leaving deep wounds.

The reasons people try to censor or restrict access haven't changed all that much over time. Books are most often attacked for being "age-inappropriate" in their use of sexually explicit or racially charged language or for expressing unorthodox political, religious or cultural views. Some challenges are brought by individual parents, others by religious right groups that target books they regard as anti-Christian.

Whatever the motive, efforts to restrict access to books deemed objectionable can polarize communities, leaving deep wounds. Classroom teachers often find themselves on the front line in these battles, yet without any real power to defend their choices or to affect the outcome—an uncomfortable place to be. . . .

Teachers no longer get fired for teaching Aldous Huxley's *Brave New World*, but most teacher contracts still don't adequately protect academic freedom, said Ann Nice, president of the Portland, Ore., Association of Teachers. Her union's contract allows members to introduce controversial materials provided they "are appropriate and relevant to course content and grade level and that balanced viewpoints on a controversial issue are presented."

That language did not prevent a months-long public debate in Portland in the fall of 2002, after a parent and two African American students challenged the way *Adventures of Huckleberry Finn* was being taught in a 9th-grade class at predominantly white Lincoln High School. Mark Twain's classic tale of a runaway slave uses the N–word more than 200 times.

The book was not removed, but student activists gathered 260 signatures on a petition to the school board asking that teachers who use it undergo sensitivity training. Even state legislators joined the debate.

Tracey Wyatt, an 18-year classroom veteran, was one of four Lincoln High English teachers who publicly supported the embattled teacher. "It could have happened to any one of us," she said.

None of the teachers stopped using *Adventures of Huckleberry Finn* as a result of the controversy, she said; in fact, her own students expressed a strong desire to read it. Lincoln teachers prepared their students by discussing Twain's use of language and describing race relations in the post-Civil War era—just as they did before the challenge flared into the headlines, Wyatt said.

High school students are ready to handle sexual, racial and other sensitive content, she said. "I don't want to bombard them. But I don't feel I need to protect them as long as I have built this safe place for them to discuss these issues. That's the key."

Wyatt added, "Some people say, 'Have them read it in college.' I don't think postponing important discussions until college is the right thing to do."

In Federal Way, Wash., 9th-grade English teacher Vince Halloran found himself in the spotlight in the spring of 2004 after 32 parents upset about sexual content in the book *Balzac and the Little Chinese Seamstress* petitioned the superintendent to remove it from the reading list. The novel by Dai Sijie, which tells the story of two youths who find a suitcase full of banned books during China's Cultural Revolution, came highly recommended by the school district's head of curriculum and instruction. After the complaint was filed, a committee that reevaluated the book gave it unanimous support.

Nonetheless, the superintendent not only agreed to remove the book but directed that, in the future, the district would provide reading lists to parents in advance and submit them to the school board for approval.

Halloran said the decision to appease the complaining parents deeply disappointed him. It also had a chilling effect, he said, "not just because teachers and students lost a precious and powerful resource, but because it seemed very clear that what mattered during this episode was who could raise the biggest stink. Reason and logic seemed to be thrown out the window."

The high court agreed that school boards have considerable discretion ... to decide what books are available in school libraries based on "community values."

Removing Books from School

Most school districts have established processes for handling complaints about course materials. If a parent objects, a teacher may assign an alternative reading. The next step typically is a formal review by a committee of principals and curriculum specialists. Finally, a parent may appeal to an elected school board and make the case for the book's removal at a public hearing where all sides get to have their say.

Complaints most often escalate into controversy when an individual teacher, principal, superintendent or school board member, responding to political pressure, bypasses that process and acts unilaterally.

That's what happened in the Savannah-Chatham County, Ga., Public Schools in 1999 after a stepfather offended by what he regarded as profanity, explicit sex and extreme violence in three books on his stepdaughter's advanced-placement reading list bypassed the teacher, principal and superintendent and went straight to the school board. At a televised meeting, he read selected passages aloud, embarrassing board members. Soon after, the principal was ordered to pull the books. Eventually, the decision was rescinded.

In 1982, the U.S. Supreme Court sent a mixed message on the issue in a New York case challenging a decision by the Island Trees Union Free School District Board of Education to order nine books removed from junior high and high school libraries.

The high court agreed that school boards have considerable discretion to determine school curricula and to decide what books are available in school libraries based on "community values." However, a majority found that it was a violation of the First Amendment for a school board to deny students access to ideas by ordering books removed from library shelves simply because board members disagreed with those ideas.

Citing a previous court ruling, Justice William Brennan wrote that students do not "shed their constitutional rights to freedom of speech or expression at the schoolhouse gate." However, the court did not address challenges to books assigned by classroom teachers.

And students are not oblivious to the message sent when a book is removed from the classroom, English teacher Halloran said.

"Students already intuit that what they are getting is divorced from and bears scant resemblance to the 'real world,'" he said. "Why not stand firm as a public institution that expresses and explores the complex range of human experience? Why be diplomatic and apologetic about the fact that we do not shy away from difficult, challenging and complex topics?"

12

Book Banning Reflects American Social Temperament

Ben MacIntyre

Ben MacIntyre writes for the London Times *and is the author of* The Napoleon of Crime: The Life and Times of Adam Worth, Master Thief.

Banning books usually has the opposite effect desired by censors: it makes the book more popular. Banned Books Week in the United States reveals the absurdity of censoring books: many of the most frequently banned items are also considered literary classics. The list of banned books also reveals a culture that continues to struggle with issues of racism, sex, and religion. Ultimately, book banning only temporarily removes books from those who want them.

Censorship of anything, for any reason whatever, anywhere in the world, at any time in history, has always been, and always will be, doomed to eventual failure.

Christian protesters thought they had successfully scuppered a national tour of *Jerry Springer: The Opera*, only to find that 21 theatres had decided to band together to ensure that the show must go on. People who like to ban things never seem to realise that the more a work of art is subjected to the outraged squeals of the censors, the more popular it becomes. "To forbid us anything is to make us have a mind for it," said Montaigne, reaching for the absinthe (banned in France in 1915; unbanned in 2001). The outlawing of *The Sa-*

Ben MacIntyre, "The American Banned List Reveals a Society with Serious Hang-Ups," *Times (UK)*, September 25, 2005. Reproduced by permission.

tanic Verses in several Islamic countries hugely boosted sales of Salman Rushdie's least distinguished book. When the ban on *Lady Chatterley's Lover* was lifted in 1960, it sold two million copies in a year: on publication day, outside Foyle's, London's largest bookshop, a queue of 400 formed before the doors opened. Most of these were men; sadly, history does not relate how many were also gardeners.

Books cannot be banned, and staunchly refuse to be burnt: as the Nazis discovered when they sought to eradicate "degenerate" literature, and as anti-Nazis discover every time they try to outlaw *The Protocols of the Elders of Zion* or *Mein Kampf*. Bash, belittle and ban the thing you hate, and it grows back even more vigorously: like bindweed, or hydra, or Anne Robinson.

Every book-banning says more about the censor than the book.

Next week is Banned Books Week in the US, when the American Library Association lists all the books that, over the previous year, people have attempted to remove from the shelves of libraries, schools and universities. This makes for sobering reading: the top ten most opposed authors in the US include J. K. Rowling (for promoting witchcraft), John Steinbeck (bad language), Maya Angelou (for sexual explicitness) and Stephen King (for being scary). In the list of the 100 most frequently challenged books of the past decade, Mark Twain's *Huckleberry Finn* comes in at No. 5 (use of the word "n—r"), J. D. Salinger *The Catcher in the Rye* at 13 (profanity, sexual references) and Alice Walker's *The Color Purple* at No. 18 (inappropriate language, sex). Astonishingly, Brett Easton Ellis's serial-killing saga *American Psycho* (a book that possibly merits banning for adjective abuse) comes romping in at No. 60.

Some of the recent attempts at censorship would be hilarious if they were not so chilling. Eureka, Illinois, removed Chaucer from its high school literature course on the grounds of sexual content. Roald Dahl's *James and the Giant Peach* was removed from some classrooms in Virginia because it promoted disobedience towards authority figures. Delightfully, *Twelfth Night* fell foul of the school board in Merrimack, New Hampshire, where the Bard stood accused of promoting an "alternative lifestyle", with all that disgusting cross-dressing. But perhaps the most remarkable act of censorious foolishness came a few years ago when four members of the Alabama State Textbook Committee called for the rejection of Anne Frank's *The Diary of a Young Girl* on the basis that it was "a real downer".

The Failure of Book Bans

The American list of opposed books reveals a society still struggling with major hang-ups about sex, race, religion and Holocaust victims who are insufficiently jolly. But it should be added that these periodic attempts to ban books have met with universal failure: indeed, every copy of Harry Potter consigned to the fire for blasphemy merely fans the flames of J. K. Rowling's popularity. But 'twas ever thus. In the 1930s Senator Smoot of Utah launched an anti-pornography campaign to the delight of Ogden Nash:

Senator Smoot (Republican, Ut.)

Is planning a ban on smut

Oh rooti-ti-toot for Smoot of Ut.

And his reverent occiput.

Smite. Smoot, smite for Ut.,

Grit your molars and do your dut.,

Gird up your l—ns, Smite h-p and th-gh,

We'll all be Kansas

By and By.

Every book-banning says more about the censor than the book. The prosecuting counsel in the *Lady Chatterley* trial could not have revealed his old-fashioned prejudices more obviously than when he asked the jury: "Is it a book you would wish your wife or servants to read?" The Greek junta laid its paranoia bare for all when, in 1967, it banned *Lysistrata*, Aristophanes' antiwar masterpiece.

Even China, so expert at banning, cannot hold back books for long. Last year two Chinese authors, Chen Guidi and Wu Chuntao, published the snappily titled *A Survey of Chinese Peasants*, an exposé of the plight of China's 800 million agricultural poor. It was banned by the Government, promptly and inevitably, but has since gone on to sell an estimated eight million copies in 30 pirate editions. Chen and Wu were last year awarded the Lettres Ulysses Award in Berlin. (Yes, that is James Joyce's *Ulysses*: banned in Britain for 14 years, as "obscene, lewd, lascivious, filthy, indecent and disgusting"; recently selected by the Modern Library as the best novel of the 20th century.)

So, as the anti-Jerry Springer brigade seeks, once again, to ban the unbannable, let us remember Thomas Bowdler (1754–1825), who took all the rude and offensive bits out of Shakespeare: "I regret that no parent could place the uncorrected book in the hands of his daughter, and therefore I have prepared the Family Shakespeare."

Bowdler's *Family Shakespeare* prospered briefly, and then vanished utterly. Bowdler survives only as a pejorative term in the *OED*, a fitting epitaph for this literary King Canute (or Smoot), who tried, and failed, to hold back the unstoppable tide.

13

Iranian Book Ban Reveals Repressive Political Regime

Kimia Sanati

Kimia Sanati is a journalist for the Inter Press Service.

While the United States worried over Iran's nuclear program at the beginning of 2007, another serious problem went unmentioned: the censorship of books and other media in Iran. A new political regime, headed by Mahmoud Ahmadinejad, even banned the majority of books approved by the previous government. Iranian writers have protested the censorship and even challenged it in court. In the meantime, censorship has bankrupted many publishers, and although a number of banned books have been secretly circulated in other countries, authors have been denied royalties. Iranians, however, have attempted to circumvent censorship by embracing new technology like the Internet Weblog.

Iran's nuclear program, an undeniably serious issue for Iranians and the rest of the world, has overshadowed the country's deplorable human rights situation, including severe censorship of books and publications.

Limiting freedom of expression in Iran covers many fields, from banning satellite TV, opposition newspapers and periodicals, student publications and books to intensive filtering of the Internet.

During the presidency of Mohammad Khatami (1997–2005), the Ministry of Culture and Islamic Guidance relaxed censorship greatly, for which it came under constant attack from hard-liners for "encouraging immorality." Yet, many works of literature and other books were published uncensored.

President Mahmoud Ahmadinejad's culture minister, whose fundamentalist views are overtly expressed, has adopted a very restrictive policy toward all areas of publication. The government is backed by a hard-liner-dominated parliament that follows the same attitude.

Out of the 659 books that had acquired publication permits under Khatami's reformist rule, 518 were found "faulty" by hard-line parliamentarians in a probe last summer. Faults cited included encouragement of illicit relations, premarital relationships and secularist views; descriptions of sex scenes; and mocking religious beliefs.

A number of prominent writers are protesting the ever-increasing pressure on writers and publishers. Among them is Mahmoud Dolatabadi, a novelist who announced in November that he would not attempt publishing any new books as long as the present attitude of the ministry's censorship department prevailed.

Another well-known novelist, Amir Hasan Cheheltan, whose novels deal with social and political issues, recently wrote a protest letter to the ministry's secretariat for the Book of the Year Award, asking that his novel, *The Persian Dawn*, be withdrawn from the list of nominations.

"There have been reports in the media that my novel has been nominated for this year's Book of the Year Award. In the past three decades, I have always been critical of the attitude of the body that holds the competition because that attitude is against the principles that I believe in.

"With great regret I must announce that as long as the publication of even one book is delayed or any book is deprived of the right of publication, my ethics will not allow me to run in the competition," the *Etemaad* newspaper quoted from Cheheltan's letter.

I may lose my publisher's license if they find out I have been interviewed by the foreign press.

The ministry's response was that he has no right to withdraw his book. "If a writer doesn't want his book to run in the Book of the Year Award competition, he shouldn't write the book. When a book is written, the writer no longer can have control over it," according to a ministry official quoted by the Fars news agency.

Fighting Censorship

Writers are resorting to the courts, too. Ebrahim Yazdi, Iran's first foreign minister after the Islamic revolution and the leader of the Freedom Movement of Iran, has long been waiting for permission to publish a collection of essays and speeches titled *Religious Intellectualism and New Challenge*. To protest what he considered deprivation of his constitutional rights, Yazdi filed a lawsuit against Culture and Islamic Guidance Minister Saffar Harandi and the director-general of the department of censorship.

"After being called to court, the director-general wrote to the publisher asking that four pages of the book be removed, but he didn't specify what the problems were. If this was done, he said, the book would be sent to the decision-making committee again for approval. I obviously didn't accept because this kind of censorship is even-against the existing laws of the Islamic Republic," Yazdi told IPS [Inter Press Service].

Emad Baghi, founder of the first Iranian society against the death penalty, is another writer whose books are routinely banned. "In spite of my ideal of maximum freedom of expression, I can put up with a certain degree of censorship. But I just can't be published even if I agree to censor myself," Baghi told IPS.

Author of more than 20 works on religion, sociology, history and the death penalty, Baghi has been denied the right to publish six books over the past few years. "This is a war waged against writers' identities. There are people among the rulers who want the identity of certain writers to be destroyed. I am one among them," he said.

Denied the printed word, the younger Iranian generation has found a new medium of expression—the Internet blog.

Publishers, too, are finding the circumstances difficult to cope with in times described by the Iranian Pen Association as one the darkest for writers in contemporary Iranian history.

"It is not just that new books are denied permission to be published. Even books that have been printed several times in the past few years are now banned. Books from any category can be banned, including modern or classical literature, political works, books on transcendental meditation and mysticism, feminist works, art books and even collections of old songs," a publisher told IPS on the condition of anonymity.

"I may lose my publisher's license if they find out I have been interviewed by the foreign press," he said.

"If the man in charge of approving publications finds anything in a book that he considers immoral or threatening to the system or views he doesn't favor himself, the book is bound to be banned. They banned a history of Iranian music because there was this picture of a female singer from ages ago in the book. Her hair wasn't covered. But that was only an excuse because we see women's hair in foreign films on state-run TV all the time," he said.

"There is a demand for most of the banned books so if a book is banned after publication or if it is published abroad, Xerox copies flood the black market. Very obviously, this deprives the writer and the publisher of their rights.

"Many publishers are going bankrupt and have to close down and writers are turning to other ways to make their living. Bookshops are now mostly surviving by selling textbooks and stationery. It's a huge cultural disaster and too serious to neglect," he added.

Denied the printed word, the younger Iranian generation has found a new medium of expression—the Internet blog. In spite of great restrictions and very intensive filtering, Iran now has the biggest number of blogs after China.

"I remember hearing about U.S. sanctions all the time since I was a child. I think everybody has gotten used to that, or the idea of an imminent U.S. attack on Iran," a passionate 23-year-old student activist and blogger told IPS.

"To be able to do as they please without facing opposition, the oppressive regime is limiting freedom of expression, even more than before. It's frightening that people are getting used to these kinds of sanctions, too."

14

Teachers Should Prepare For Book Challenges

Sharon Cromwell

Sharon Cromwell is a regular contributor to Education World.

Censorship battles over controversial books in public schools have led to bitter debates within communities. Censorship is a complex issue. While the Supreme Court has supported a school board's right to choose curriculum materials for schools, the court has also stressed the importance of community standards. For school boards, the best method of handling controversial material is to have a clearly stated policy. School boards may also wish to ask for parental participation. Even with clear policies, controversies erupt. When they do, a school should attempt to explain the issue, provide a copy of the school's policies, and inform the complainant of the review process.

What books should be taught in schools? It sounds like a simple question but the answer can be complex.

Challenges to curriculum content have torn apart communities. On the one hand, advocates of banning certain books maintain that children in grades K–12 will be harmed if we don't protect them from inappropriate materials. Opponents are equally heated in insisting that censorship of books and other curriculum materials violates the academic freedom and diversity of thought protected by the U.S. Constitution.

Among the classic works of literature banned from schools over the years have been Shakespeare's *Hamlet*, Nathaniel

Sharon Cromwell, "Banning Books From the Classroom: How to Handle Cries for Censorship," *Education World*, www.education-world.com/a_curr/curr031.shtml, September 23, 2005. © 2005 Education World, Inc. Reproduced by permission.

Hawthorne's *Scarlet Letter,* and Mark Twain's *The Adventures of Huckleberry Finn.* An American Civil Liberties Union report lists among the most frequently banned or challenged books of 1997 R. L. Stine's *Goosebumps* series, *I Know Why the Caged Bird Sings* by Maya Angelou, and *Catcher in the Rye* by J. D. Salinger.

A report by the National School Boards Association (NSBA) found that challenges of school materials are common throughout the United States. Those challenges frequently work; nearly one-third result in materials being withdrawn from schools or their use curtailed.

During Banned Books Week, people are exhorted to fight against banning and censorship. Yet do opponents of banning books believe that *any* book is appropriate for teaching in school? And where should the line be drawn between books that are appropriate and inappropriate? A number of experts have explored these and related questions of censorship.

The Meaning of Censorship and Legal Trends

Censorship is "the removal, suppression, or restricted circulation of literary, artistic or educational materials . . . on the grounds that these are morally or otherwise objectionable in light of the standards applied by the censor," writes Henry Reichman in *Censorship and Selection, Issues and Answers for Schools.* According to definitions like this, observers point out, many decisions made by school boards about what can be taught in schools might be seen as acts of censorship.

Challenges to materials in school curricula, according to *Censorship of Curriculum Materials,* by JeanMarie Aurnague-DeSpain and Alan Bass, generally arise in the following areas:

- sex and drug education

- literature showing children challenging parents and authorities

- teaching evolution without reference to creationism

- showing women behaving in nontraditional ways

- "invasions of privacy"—projects requiring students to share personal information.

To avoid controversy, school boards need clearly stated policies delineating how materials are selected.

Supreme Court cases that deal with censorship issues show a broad trend toward supporting the schools, but they also caution educators to remain aware of values, including minority values, in the communities they serve. Experts have cited the First Amendment of the Constitution as protecting both students' rights to know and teachers' rights to academic freedom. At the same time, legal experts argue, parents have the right to protest books or materials that they consider damaging to their children.

In a landmark censorship case, *Island Trees Union Free High School v. Pico* (1982), the Court asserted that the "Constitution does not permit the official suppression of ideas," and the banned books were returned to school shelves. In this and other cases, the Court seems to allow school boards a rather free hand with curriculum materials.

In the Pico case, Justice Brennan's plurality opinion stated that a basis for resolving censorship conflicts over school materials could rest upon the use of "established . . . unbiased procedures for the review of controversial materials" at the local level.

Avoiding and Handling Controversy

To avoid controversy, school boards need clearly stated policies delineating how materials are selected. Selection policies should weigh the viewpoints of various groups in the community and be implemented by professionals. Those developing selection policies must consider community and parental concerns and demonstrate acceptance of our national diversity, asserts Reichman. If selection policy ignores minority rights, censorship issues may arise. And school materials should not be selected for partisan political reasons.

To develop a community consensus and prevent cries for censorship, Larry Mikulecky . . . recommends several strategies:

- Ask parents to contribute to developing school reading programs.

- Give recommended, rather than required, reading lists.

- Have files of professional reviews that support materials.

- In collective bargaining agreements, negotiate clauses that protect academic freedom and call for agreed-on selection processes.

- Discourage the concept that only one text can be used to teach a specific theme.

When controversy flares up despite efforts to avoid it, there are ways of handling it to minimize damage. In "Censorship of Curriculum Materials," JeanMarie Aurnague-DeSpain and Alan Baas say, "good internal communications and public relations offer the best way to avoid unnecessary controversy."

Several experts recommend the following process, says "Censorship of Curriculum Materials":

- Meet with the complainant and attempt to resolve the issue.

- If that fails, request a written complaint detailing the questionable material, the bad effect it is thought to have on students, and what replacement materials are suggested.

- Give the complainant a copy of published district policies for controversial materials and explain the procedure to be followed.

- Have a review committee provide the school board with a final report.

- Inform the complainant of the review process and when committee meetings are slated.

- Provide an appeals process.

- While the complaint is being explored, keep the controversial material available, except possibly to the student whose family has filed a challenge.

School boards are legally responsible for what is taught in a district, according to U.S. courts in general. The board delegates power to school officials and so is held responsible for school policies.

In summary, the NSBA report states that "the challenge is not to avoid censorship, but to meet it head on with adequate policies and procedures that provide an open forum for deciding what should—or should not—take place in public schools."

15

Book Destruction Controls Ideology

Rebecca Knuth

Rebecca Knuth is an associate professor in the Library and Information Science Program at the University of Hawaii.

In the 20th century, fascist and communist ideologues attempted to destroy democratic and humanistic thought by destroying books. Books disseminate ideas, and many of these ideas form cultural myths and identities; censoring books, then, is one way to eliminate ideas and myths that oppose a particular ideologue's philosophy. A number of modern conflicts, like World War II, pitted ideologues against humanists. Ideologues believed that destroying offending books and libraries—both their own and those of an enemy—encouraged the correct thinking of the reigning regime.

> "Utopias have their value—nothing so wonderfully expands the imaginative horizons of human potentialities—but as guides to conduct they can prove literally fatal. Heraclitus was right, things cannot stand still."

(Berlin 1991, 15)

In the most general sense, one could say that the ultra-nationalists and Communists of the twentieth century effectively replaced traditional systems of ethics and morality by a single means: the leveraging of ideology. Nationalism and so-

Rebecca Knuth, *Libricide: The Regime-Sponsored Destruction of Books and Libraries in the Twentieth Century*. Westport, CT: Praeger Publishers, 2003, pp. 236–38. Copyright © 2003 by Rebecca Knuth. All rights reserved. Reproduced by permission of Greenwood Publishing Group, Inc., Westport, CT.

cialism, in themselves compelling belief systems, were transformed by merciless leaders into totalistic dogmas that reduced what is sacred to a single notion of predestined collective potential. Familial loyalties were subordinated to loyalty to the state. A sociopolitical environment was engineered to snuff out alternative ideas. Violence was instituted as necessary, and even desirable, in the quest to maintain the totalitarian structures that would deliver a purified and transformed society.

Fueling the impulse toward violence was the ideologues' conviction that enemies—animate or inanimate, a person, even a book—surrounded them. When a book's content contradicted an ideologue's dominance over ideas and seemed to support cosmopolitanism, democracy, or humanism, that book was labeled a tool of the enemy and in itself, a dangerous thing. Such a book, therefore, became a candidate for censorship, which ran the gamut from blacklisting to burning or pulping. Similarly, when libraries were identified as hindering ideological transformation and impeding progress toward the desired utopia, they were attacked and sometimes eliminated, along with their human possessors. Perhaps the most astonishing part of this phenomenon was the inclusion of a nation's own possessions as enemies to the cause. The Nazis first censored and destroyed those *German* books that they considered problematic, then destroyed the books of those they considered pathological (the Jews), inferior (the Poles), and resistant (the British). When ideological fervor intensified in China, the Communist radicals destroyed classic *Chinese* texts and intellectuals and in Tibet, both texts and resistant Tibetans. With progress narrowly defined as achieving ideological goals, print materials often came to be associated with cultural or political intransigence and their destruction a war effort on the same two fronts. The violence and public nature of destruction often obscured the fact that the ruin was a practical means of destroying information that contradicted the myths of the regime or substantiated the claims of other ethnic or political groups to resources and territory.

Books were destroyed as part of the process of homogenizing discourse, suppressing individualism in the interest of the collective, and co-opting or purging the intellectuals.

Books as Ideas

Books were destroyed as part of the process of homogenizing discourse, suppressing individualism in the interest of the collective, and co-opting or purging the intellectuals. The goal of extremist regimes was complete control, and books and libraries were compromised by their association with humanism, the creed of enemy democracies. Indeed, the twentieth-century ideologues despised humanists, who valued books and libraries for precisely those qualities that pitted them against ideologues. Regardless of their individual agendas, books ultimately, by their very existence and coexistence with the entirety of the world's print literature, support individualism, pluralism, creativity, rationalism, freedom of information, critical thinking, and intellectual freedom. The ideologue must reject traditional knowledge in order to look to the future, while the humanist actively seeks inspiration from the past. Humanists believe that written materials are fundamental to the maintenance and progress of culture; ideologues seek to politicize and overturn existing culture. Ideologues view libraries as problematic, their potential as instruments of indoctrination compromised by their humanistic or reactionary nature and ability to pose alternate realities or ideas. World War II was fought between ideologues and humanists, and books and libraries played no small role. The jubilant Nazi book burnings and the ensuing wartime devastation of cultural institutions throughout the world resulted in the United Nations' orientation toward the preservation of humanism.

The cultivation of a world in which cultural resources are safe became a declared goal of both and technology by preserving and disseminating the information necessary for scientific inquiry, technological development, and the systematic advancement of knowledge. These functions, which made libraries the quintessential representation of humanism, were problematic for extremists. For example, Chinese Communist radicals of the 1960s and 1970s wanted industrialization based not on scientific and technological expertise but on revolutionary will and zeal. Libraries suffered as a consequence. The Nazis sought to rationalize racism, and German libraries flourished only when they aligned with this goal.

Extremists need to control humanist institutions and transform them from cultural resources into political tools, part of the overall machine of the revolution. Ideologues censor and then reconstruct their own libraries and those of conquered enemies, or they destroy books or entire libraries outright because they fear the connection between libraries and alternate belief systems, especially humanism, which allow for pluralism. Books and libraries are destroyed not only because of their functions within a society, but because, by the twentieth century, books, libraries, and all intellectual pursuits had become clearly linked to humanism. Their destruction was part of an overall system of eliminating the influence of humanism in the sociopolitical arena, particularly as concerned intellectuals, scholarship, science, history, and foreign relations.

16

Book Destruction Destroys Cultural Identity

Nicholas A. Basbanes

Nicholas A. Basbanes has published multiple books including A Gentle Madness: Bibliophiles, Bibliomanes, and the Eternal Passion for Books.

In 1992, Serbian nationalists bombarded the National Library and University of Bosnia and Herzegovina. As a result, most of the books and materials in the library, including many rare manuscripts, were destroyed. While shelling a library may seem like an accident of war, the destruction of the National Library was only one of several libraries that the Serbian nationalists targeted. In essence, the Serbian forces attempted to erase ideas they disagreed with, eliminating the foundation of an enemy's cultural identity.

In the early evening hours of August 25, 1992, Serbian nationalist soldiers nested in the craggy hills surrounding the besieged city of Sarajevo trained their artillery pieces on a graceful building that for four decades had functioned admirably as home to the National and University Library of Bosnia and Herzegovina. Shortly after 10 P.M., the gunmen opened fire with a barrage of incendiary shells from four elevated positions, using a proven targeting technique known as bracketing to measure the precise range for their volleys. Before long spotters were reporting direct hits on the structure's most prominent features, a stained-glass skylight and a rounded copper cupola, and within minutes the architectural landmark known to local residents as Vijecnica (Town Hall) was spewing flames high into the night sky. Attempts to save the irreplaceable contents were heroic, but in the end hopelessly futile. A makeshift crew that had ventured inside the doomed structure on the ground floor barely escaped serious injury when a band of narrow support columns in the old reading room began to explode from the intense heat, causing a section of the roof to come crashing down in a cascade of flaming rubble. Hampered by low pressure in the water mains, firefighters watched helplessly as the north wall collapsed and as the priceless patrimony of a beleaguered people went up in smoke.

Fueled by fifteen thousand meters of wooden shelving and a collection of books estimated to have numbered 1.5 million volumes, the fire smoldered for three days, filling the hot summer sky with clouds of searing fragments that one witness described as a blizzard of sooty black snow. Ignoring the threat of sniper fire coming in from the mountains, volunteers set up a web of human chains and removed 100,000 volumes from the stricken building. An official casualty list released by Bosnia's Ministry of Health disclosed that 14 people were killed and 126 wounded in Sarajevo on the day the library was attacked. Listed among the victims was Aida Buturovic, a thirty-two-year-old cataloger struck by shrapnel from a mortar shell while returning home after a frenzied night of saving books at the library; she died instantly from her wounds.

In addition to mass murder, the methodical obscenity used by the Serbs known as ethnic cleansing during the conflict included the destruction of cultural artifacts.

In addition to mass murder, the methodical obscenity used by the Serbs known as ethnic cleansing during the conflict included the destruction of cultural artifacts, and represented what horrified observers called a systematic "attack on memory" meant to eradicate every trace of a despised neighbor's existence. Killing the people, in other words, was viewed by the perpetrators as little more than a productive beginning to the larger task at hand. "What is more important in a library than anything else—than everything else—is the fact that it exists," the poet-librarian Archibald MacLeish proclaimed in 1971, an assertion that underscored how essential national repositories are to preserving a people's touchstones with their past. Losses at the Sarajevo library were especially crippling, since the holdings represented a common heritage that Muslims, Serbians, and Croatians had shared for more than four hundred years, gathered together after World War II under one roof when the new national library was organized, and the books and archives of the Bosnian Serb community known as Prosvjeta, and the Bosnian Muslim cultural society known as Napredak, became part of the combined collections. Among other materials incinerated were 155,000 rare books and manuscripts, substantial holdings of archival materials, musical scores, historical photographs, prints, and ephemera, along with complete sets of magazines, literary journals, and newspapers published in Bosnia-Herzegovina since the mid-nineteenth century. The entire periodicals collection was lost too, as were the library's card catalogs.

If the 1992 bombardment had been an isolated incident ... Serbian denials of having deliberately marked books for destruction might not have met with such disbelief throughout the world.

Built on the banks of the Miljacka River at the edge of the Ottoman quarter near the center of town, the building originally functioned as a municipal center for the city of Sarajevo, and was completed in 1896 when Bosnia and Herzegovina were part of the Austro-Hungarian Empire. Designed in a pseudo-Moorish style, Vijecnica (pronounced VYECH-neetsa) complemented the graceful mosques that distinguished the city's elegant skyline. On June 28, 1914, Archduke Ferdinand of Austria and his wife, Sophie, were assassinated by a Serbian terrorist after leaving a reception in the building, the event that set in motion the outbreak of World War I.

Established in 1945, the National Library was stocked with books from several collections that had survived the ravages of world war, and moved into the old town hall in 1951. Once the institution was designated official depository for works published in Bosnia and Herzegovina and the territory of Yugoslavia, its holdings began to grow rapidly. With formation of the University of Sarajevo in 1957, it became an academic research facility as well, and began an active exchange of materials with many of the world's major institutions. A number of important manuscript archives were acquired during this period, including those of the Croatian poet Silvije Stahimir Kranjcevic and the Serbian poet Aleksa Simic.

If the 1992 bombardment had been an isolated incident in the three-and-a-half-year war that claimed ten thousand lives in Sarajevo alone, Serbian denials of having deliberately marked books for destruction might not have met with such disbelief throughout the world. But three months earlier, the Oriental Institute in Sarajevo, repository for one of Europe's most extensive collections of Islamic and Jewish manuscripts, was also targeted by the Serbs. Lost in that assault were 5,263 bound manuscripts in Arabic, Persian, Turkish, Hebrew, and a local Serbo-Croat-Bosnian Arabic script known as *alhamijado* or *adzamijski*, along with thousands of documents from the Ottoman era. Other attacks were carried out on the library of the Museum of Herzegovina, the Archives of Herzegovina, the library of the Roman Catholic Archbishopric in Mostar, and the Orthodox monastery in Zitomislic.

A year and a half after the National Library was destroyed, the American journalist Mark Danner asked Dr. Radovan Karadzic, the leader of the Bosnian Serbs, how a practicing psychiatrist, a published poet who once taught Shakespeare, could justify destroying such an irreplaceable cultural legacy. "It was a Christian building, you know, from the Austro-Hungarian period, and so the Muslims hated it," he replied, insisting that the Muslims had ignited the building themselves in an attempt "to gain the sympathy" of the world. "Only Christian books were burned," he claimed. "The others were removed." He was equally dismissive of matters relating to all the other charges as well, even any culpability for initiating mass killings. "The Serbs did not invent ethnic cleansing," he said. "The Croats did, in World War II."

Investigating what he described as "culturecide" during the war in Bosnia, British journalist Robert Fisk reported seeing widespread destruction of historic buildings and precious artifacts throughout the region formerly known as Yugoslavia. "It is sometimes a shock to find something that has survived," he wrote, noting his astonishment that the greatest treasure of the badly damaged sixteenth-century Karadjoz-Bey mosque, a fragile Koran handwritten and illuminated in gold in Baghdad during the 1300s, escaped incineration only because it had been placed for safekeeping beneath the floorboards of a grimy outhouse. "You have to understand that the cultural identity of a population represents its survival in the future," Jan Boeles, head of the Dutch delegation to the European Community Monitor Mission investigating possible war crimes, told Fisk. "When the Serbs blow up the mosque of a village and destroy its graveyards and the foundations of the graveyards and mosque and level them all off with a bulldozer, no one can ever, ever tell this was a Muslim village. This is the murder of a people's cultural identity."

Organizations to Contact

The editors have compiled the following list of organizations concerned with the issues debated in this book. The descriptions are derived from materials provided by the organizations. All have publications or information available for interested readers. The list was compiled on the date of publication of the present volume; the information provided here may change. Be aware that many organizations take several weeks or longer to respond to inquiries, so allow as much time as possible.

American Civil Liberties Union
125 Broad St., 18th Floor, New York, NY   10004
(212) 549-2500 • fax: (212) 549-2646
e-mail: aclu@aclu.org
Web site: www.aclu.org

The American Civil Liberties Union (ACLU) is a national organization that defends Americans' civil rights as guaranteed in the U.S. Constitution. It advocates for freedom of all forms of speech, including pornography, flag-burning, and political protest. The ACLU offers numerous reports, fact sheets, and policy statements on free speech issues, which are freely available on its Web site. Some of these publications include "Free Speech Under Fire," "Freedom of Expression," and, for students, "Ask Sybil Liberty About Your Right to Free Expression."

American Library Association
50 E. Huron Street, Chicago, IL   60611
(800) 545-2433 • fax: (312) 440-9374
e-mail: ala@ala.org
Web site: www.ala.org

The American Library Association (ALA) is the United States' primary professional organization for librarians. Through its Office for Intellectual Freedom (OIF), the ALA supports free access to libraries and library materials. The OIF also monitors and opposes efforts to ban books from libraries. Its publications, which are freely available on its Web site, include "Intellectual Freedom and Censorship Q & A," the "Library Bill of Rights," and the "Freedom to Read Statement."

Brennan Center for Justice

New York University School of Law, New York, NY 10013
(212) 998-6733 • fax: (212) 995-4550
Web site: www.fepproject.org

The Brennan Center for Justice is a non-partisan public policy and law institute that focuses on the fundamental issues of democracy and justice. The Brennan Center for Justice's work ranges from voting rights to redistricting reform, from access to the courts to presidential power in the fight against terrorism. The Brennan Center combines scholarship, legislative and legal advocacy, and communications to win meaningful, measurable change in the public sector.

Canadian Association for Free Expression

P.O. Box 332 Station 'B', Etobicoke, Ontario
  M9W 5L3 Canada
(905) 897-7221 • fax: (905) 277-3914
e-mail: cafe@canadafirst.net
Web site: www.canadianfreespeech.com

The Canadian Association for Free Expression (CAFE), one of Canada's leading civil liberties groups, works to strengthen the freedom of speech and freedom of expression provisions in the Canadian Charter of Rights and Freedoms. It lobbies politicians and researches threats to freedom of speech. Publications include specialized reports, leaflets, and *The Free Speech Monitor*, which is published ten times per year.

Family Research Council

801 G Street NW, Washington, DC 20001
(202) 393-2100 • fax: (202) 393-2134
Web site: www.frc.org

The Family Research Council (FRC) is a faith-based organization that seeks to promote marriage and family. It believes that pornography harms women, children, and families, and therefore the FRC seeks to strengthen current obscenity laws. It publishes a variety of books, policy papers, fact sheets, and other materials, including the brochure "Dealing with Pornography: A Practical Guide for Protecting Your Family and Your Community" and the book *Protecting Your Child in an X-Rated World: What You Need to Know to Make a Difference.*

First Amendment Center at Vanderbilt University
1207 18th Ave. S., Nashville, TN   37212
(615) 727-1600 • fax: (615) 727-1319
e-mail: info@fac.org
Web site: www.firstamendmentcenter.org

The First Amendment Center works to preserve and protect First Amendment freedoms through information and education. The Center serves as a forum for the study and exploration of free-expression issues, including freedom of speech, of the press, and of religion, and the rights to assemble and to petition the government.

Foundation for Individual Rights in Education
601 Walnut St., Suite 510, Philadelphia, PA   19106
(215) 717-3473 • fax: (215) 717-3440
e-mail: fire@thefire.org
Web site: www.thefire.org

The Foundation for Individual Rights in Education (FIRE) was founded in 1999 to defend the rights of students and professors at American colleges and universities. The group advocates for and provides legal assistance to students and professors who feel that their individual rights, particularly their rights to free speech, have been violated. Its publications include *FIRE's Guide to Free Speech on Campus* and "Spotlight: The Campus Freedom Resource," which contains information about speech codes at specific colleges and universities.

Freedom Forum

1101 Wilson Blvd., Arlington, VA   22209
(703) 528-0800 • fax: (703) 284-3770
e-mail: news@freedomforum.org
Web site: www.freedomforum.org

The Freedom Forum was founded in 1991 to defend a free press and free speech. It operates the Newseum (a museum of news and the news media) and the First Amendment Center, which works to educate the public about free speech and other First Amendment issues. Its publications include an annual "State of the First Amendment" survey, and the First Amendment Center maintains on its Web site a "First Amendment Library" that serves as a clearinghouse for judicial, legislative, and other material on First Amendment freedoms.

Morality in Media

475 Riverside Dr., Suite 239, New York, NY   10115
(212) 870-3222 • fax: (212) 870-2765
e-mail: mim@moralityinmedia.org
Web site: www.moralityinmedia.org

Morality in Media (MIM) is a national interfaith organization that fights obscenity and indecency in the media. It works to educate the public on obscenity issues and maintains the National Obscenity Law Center, a clearinghouse of legal materials on obscenity law. Its publications include the reports "Stranger in the House," "Pornography's Effects on Adults and Children," and the bimonthly *Morality in Media Newsletter*.

National Coalition Against Censorship

275 Seventh Avenue, New York, NY   10001
(212) 807-6222 • fax: (212) 807-6245
e-mail: ncac@ncac.org
Web site: www.ncac.org

The National Coalition against Censorship (NCAC) is an alliance of national not-for-profit organizations, including literary, artistic, religious, educational, professional, labor, and civil liberties groups. The coalition works to defend freedom of thought, inquiry, and expression and to fight censorship. Its Web site provides access to press releases, legal briefs, and Congressional testimony on censorship issues.

National Coalition for the Protection of Children and Families

800 Compton Rd., Suite 9224, Cincinnati, OH   45231
(513) 521-6 227 • fax: (513) 521-6337
e-mail: ncpcf@nationalcoalition.org
Web site: www.nationalcoalition.org

The National Coalition for the Protection of Children and Families is a Christian organization that encourages traditional sexual ethics and fights pornography. It encourages strong regulation of adult bookstores and the use of Internet filters in public libraries. Its publications include the *Library Protection Plan* and the booklet *Pornography: The Deconstruction of Human Sexuality*.

Parents against Bad Books in Schools

4326 Ferry Landing Rd., Alexandria, VA   22309
(703) 360-8853 • fax: (703) 360-8853
e-mail: pabbis@pabbis.com
Web site: www.pabbis.com

Parents against Bad Books in Schools (PABBIS) promotes the removal of controversial material from public schools and is located in Virginia. PABBIS believes that schools should not infringe on a family's religious beliefs and values. In an effort to sustain parents' right to protect children from offensive material, PABBIS supports parental activism in regard to books within school systems that offend individual values.

People for the American Way

2000 M Street, NW, Suite 400, Washington, DC   20036
(202) 467-4999 • fax: (202) 293-2672
e-mail: pfaw@pfaw.org
Web site: www.pfaw.org

PFAW works to promote citizen participation in democracy and safeguard the principles of the U.S. Constitution, including the right to free speech. It publishes a variety of fact sheets, articles, and position statements on its Web site and distributes the e-mail newsletter *Freedom to Learn Online.*

Townhall

1901 N. Moore Street, Suite 205, Arlington, VA   22209
(703) 294-6046
e-mail: info@townhall.com
Web site: www.townhall.com

Townhall was launched in 1995 as the first conservative web community. Townhall split off from the Heritage Foundation in 2005, expanding the scope of its mission to inform, empower, and mobilize citizens for political change. Townhall pulls together news and political commentary from a vast array of partner organizations and columnists.

Bibliography

Books

Margaret Bald	*Literature Suppressed on Religious Grounds.* New York: Facts on File, 2006.
Paul S. Boyer	*Purity in Print: Book Censorship in America from the Gilded Age to the Computer Age.* Madison, WI: University of Wisconsin Press, 2002.
Cathy Byrd and Susan Richmond, eds.	*Potentially Harmful: The Art of American Censorship.* Atlanta, GA: Ernest G. Welch School of Art & Design Gallery, Georgia State University, 2006.
Joan DelFattore	*What Johnny Shouldn't Read: Textbook Censorship in America.* New Haven, CT: Yale University Press, 1992.
Nina Felshin and Richard Meyer	*Potentially Harmful: The Art of American Censorship.* Atlanta, GA: Georgia State University, 2006.
Nicholas J. Karolides, Margaret Bald, and Dawn B. Sova	*120 Banned Books: Censorship Histories Of World Literature.* New York: Checkmark Books, 2005.
Nicholas J. Karolides	*Literature Suppressed on Political Grounds.* New York: Facts on File, 2006.

Robert C. Post, ed.	*Censorship and Silencing: Practices of Cultural Regulation.* Los Angeles: Getty Trust Publications, 1998.
Diane Ravitch	*The Language Police: How Pressure Groups Restrict What Students Learn.* New York: Knopf, 2003.
Salman Rushdie	*The Satanic Verses.* New York: Picador, 2000.
Pat R. Scales	*Teaching Banned Books: 12 Guides for Young Readers.* Chicago: American Library Association, 2001.
Lawrence Soley	*Censorship, Inc.: The Corporate Threat to Free Speech in the United States.* New York: Monthly Review Press, 2002.
Dawn B. Sova	*Literature Suppressed on Sexual Grounds.* New York: Facts on File, 2006.
Dawn B. Sova	*Literature Suppressed on Social Grounds.* New York: Facts on File, 2006.
Els van der Plas, Malu Halasa, and Marlous Willemsen, eds.	*Creating Spaces of Freedom: Culture in Defiance.* London: Saqi Books, 2002.

Periodicals

Tammy Alhadef	"Banned Books Spark a Defense of Literature," *Pueblo Chieftain*, September 27, 2006.

Colette Bancroft — "I'm in Vonnegut's Cult," *St. Petersburg Times*, April 15, 2007.

Kelsey Bradbury — "Authors of Teen Novels Defend Their Right to Tackle Tough Subjects," *Buffalo News*, September 27, 2006.

G. McLeod Bryan — "Banning of Books Had Long-Reaching Effect," *Winston-Salem Journal*, November 18, 2006.

Jennifer Chou — "Banned in Beijing; China's Censors Send a Clear Message," *Weekly Standard*, February 1, 2007.

Blaise Cronin — "Burned Any Good Books Lately?," *Library Journal*, February 15, 2003.

"Books on the Hook" — *Current Events*, vol. 20, March 5, 2007.

Jameson Currier — "Publishing Notes," *Lambda Book Report*, January–March 2005.

Allison Eck — "Teachers, Students Weigh in on 'Banned Books Week,'" *Buffalo News*, September 27, 2006.

Justin Fenton — "Author Banned After Nudity Remark," *Baltimore Sun*, April 26, 2007.

Sally Fiedler — "Where Reading and Writing Are Punishable By Death," *Buffalo News*, August 27, 2006.

John Fraser — "Through the Centuries, the Books Never Stay Banned," *Globe & Mail*, February 12, 2005.

Barbara L. Fredricksen "This Week, Curl Up With Books That Are Banned," *St. Petersburg Times*, September 25, 2004.

Stephen Gillers "Free the *Ulysses* Two," *Nation*, February 19, 2007.

Kelly Milner Halls "Should These Books Be Banned?," *Denver Post*, September 26, 2004.

Nicole Yunger Halpern "Read a Banned Book This Week," *Tampa Tribune*, September 28, 2006.

Hillel Italie "Attempts to Ban Books From Libraries on the Rise," *Wisconsin State Journal*, September 14, 2005.

Jane Macartney "Online Rebellion Forces Censors to Back Down on Banned Books," *Times* (U.K.), March 16, 2007.

Jack Malvern and Will Pavia "Foreign Writers Stabbed in the Back," *Times*, January 4, 2006.

MEED: Middle East Economic Digest "Media Revolution: The Explosion of Arab Media Has Been Hailed as a Spur to Innovation and the Key to the Knowledge-Based Economies of the Future—But Censorship Remains a Fact of Life" vol. 51, no. 16, April 20, 2007.

Sara Nelson "Wal-Mart Refuses Carlin's New Book," *New York Post*, October 28, 2004.

Thomas G. Palaima "A School's Wise Stand Against Book Banning," *Austin American-Statesman*, October 5, 2005.

Reading Eagle   "Harry Potter Books Shouldn't Be Banned," October 13, 2006.

Evelyn Ryan   "Banned Books Week: Unique Prestige Bestowed on Many Well-Known Authors," *Dominion Post*, September 25, 2006.

Laura T. Ryan   "Persecuted Pages: Libraries, Bookstores, Celebrate Freedom and Reading Choices during Banned Books Week," *Post-Standard* (Syracuse, NY), September 24, 2006.

Jeff Webb   "This Week, Try a By-the-Book Way to Protect Freedom," *St. Petersburg Times*, September 28, 2005.

Chris Smith   "To Read Or Not to Read (Should
Wilson   School Librarians Ban Books?)," *Owl*, November 2006.

Rachel Baruch   "Libraries Campaign for Freedom
Yackley   From Bans," *Daily Herald* (Arlington Heights, IL), September 26, 2004.

Index